Praise for *The Bostonian*

'From grassroots insight into local Boson politics to informed analysis of the national polarised picture to transatlantic love stories, this book is entertaining, informative and passionate. A must-read for fans of US politics, Irish-American relations and immigration tales.'

CAITRÍONA PERRY, journalist, broadcaster and author

'The political journey of Larry Donnelly's family, and in particular his own political and cultural odyssey, is a roadmap for the Irish immigrant experience in America, where tribal loyalties eventually give way to demographic realities. His journey back to Ireland, where he made his life, reveals that the phenomenon of what social scientists call 'third-generation return', in which the grandchildren of immigrants identify with the old country, is rooted in DNA as much as cultural identity. Larry Donnelly's ability to see America through Irish eyes, and Ireland through American eyes, is remarkable and revealing – as much a social history as a personal memoir.'

KEVIN CULLEN, *Boston Globe*

'For those of us who know him as a public-spirited legal academic and political pundit in Ireland, this part-memoir, part-political-reflection is an intriguing insight into Larry Donnelly's backstory growing up and qualifying as a lawyer in Boston before some twists and turns of fate brought him to Ireland. The book is framed with his political perspectives. Not afraid to advance strong opinions, Donnelly is respectful of the political process and those who engage in it, whether he agrees with them or not. His thoughtful and optimistic punditry style that has become familiar to us over the years makes this book an easy and worthwhile read.'

NOELINE BLACKWELL, CEO, Dublin Rape Crisis Centre

'Boston politics is a never-ending story. Larry Donnelly shares his fascinating part in it in an equally profound, humorous and revealing way. You don't have to be Irish to enjoy it!'

CAL THOMAS, syndicated columnist

THE
BOSTONIAN

LIFE IN AN IRISH-AMERICAN
POLITICAL FAMILY

Larry Donnelly

Gill Books

Gill Books
Hume Avenue
Park West
Dublin 12
www.gillbooks.ie

Gill Books is an imprint of M.H. Gill and Co.

© Larry Donnelly 2021
9780717190423

Edited by Sheila Armstrong
Proofread by Sally Vince
Design and print origination by O'K Graphic Design, Dublin
Printed by CPI Group (UK) Ltd, Croydon, CR0 4YY

This book is typeset in 12/18 pt Sabon.

This book is dedicated in loving memory to my parents,
Lawrence P. ('Larry') Donnelly (30 April 1934–15 April 2021)
and Mary (Flanigan) Donnelly (8 December 1934–6 February
2008). Dad was my hero. He taught me everything he knew
about politics and more. Mum was the most unselfish person
I have ever known, who treated everyone she met with great
kindness and respect. Somehow, she put up with the three men
in our house. I couldn't have asked for a better mother
or father. Words cannot express how much I wish they were
alive to read the pages that follow.

CONTENTS

PART THREE – THE VIEW FROM THE CENTRE

Author's Note

In the immortal words of Ferris Bueller, 'life moves pretty fast.' Nowhere is this truer than in the world of politics. This book accounts for all developments in Ireland and the United States as of June 2021. In the likely event that there have been significant happenings since, I believe that strong clues as to what my take on them would be can be found in this book.

An Introduction to Politics on the Ground Floor

'Welcome to the family business, kid!'

My father bellowed out these words from our front door and they rang in my ears as I strolled somewhat apprehensively down the street I grew up on, armed with a clipboard, two pens and several sheets of officially headed paper from the town clerk's office. I was on a mission to obtain a mere 25 signatures from neighbours in order to get my name on the ballot for the lowliest of elected positions in Massachusetts local government: representative town meeting member.

I was just 22 years old, having completed an undergraduate degree and moved back to my family home while pursuing a Juris Doctor (Doctor of Law) degree in Boston. Politics had long been my passion, euphemistically, and my obsession, in reality, from an unusually young age. And this was the first actual foray 'in the arena' for me. It was something I had long been encouraged to do and had expressed a serious interest in, but the idea of it had always been far more romantic than the drudgery – setting out to knock on familiar and unfamiliar doors, looking to obtain the assistance of those who answered on that Saturday in the winter of 1997.

Although Dad never sugar-coated what any political candidacy entailed, I had shrugged it off as no big deal beforehand. Like many children, sons in particular, I should have listened more carefully to my father. Dad had more experience than almost anyone in this regard. His mother's side of the family had been involved in electoral politics in the city of Boston and the state of Massachusetts since emigrating from the west of Ireland around the start of the 20th century.

My father's great-uncles, Frank and Johnny Kelly, were legendary graduates of the old school. As a unit, they were once described as rather unsavoury characters, who the then-ruling Boston Brahmin WASPish class 'feared would get control of [what had always been their] city and run it into the ground'.[1] The Boston Brahmins were the descendants of mainly British landowners who were among the first people to come to the 'new world' and who retained a stranglehold on wealth and power in the city. They were often sceptical of new immigrants, the Irish in particular. Frank was, in his era, the youngest-ever Boston City Councillor elected. He later served as the Lieutenant Governor and Attorney General of Massachusetts. Johnny was also a Boston City Councillor and was eventually chosen by his peers to be president of that body.

In the next generation, Dad's younger brother, Brian Donnelly, my godfather, spent three terms in the Massachusetts House of Representatives, seven terms in the United States House of Representatives and subsequently worked closely with Ambassador Madeleine Albright at the United Nations,

1 Thomas O'Connor, *Building a New Boston: Politics and Urban Renewal, 1950–1970* (Northeastern University Press, 1995).

2

prior to being appointed United States Ambassador to Trinidad and Tobago by President Bill Clinton.

In short, politics really was the family business and, since I was young, I had – with no small amount of ambition or ego – envisaged myself as the one destined to carry on a proud tradition. One thing Dad constantly stressed was the respect he had for politicians who started at the bottom and worked their way up. As such, he wouldn't have me trying to parlay what was a strong name brand into skipping entry-level politics.

In truth, however, there was another, far bigger obstacle to my going to the front of the queue. It was one of my own making. And it's one that may shock those who have heard me talk or read what I've written about American politics over the past two decades.

I was a fully signed-up, card-carrying member of the Republican Party.

Strangely, it was my father's oft-expressed disgust with the Democratic Party that at least partly led me to wilfully abandon a central institution in our lives and in the lives of so many others in the Boston Irish community. Above all, it was the huge distance that had sprung up between the party and the other main institution for most Boston Irish, the Roman Catholic Church, which gave rise to the discontent. My father was far from alone in finding himself isolated from national and local Democrats who embraced the socially liberal agenda that rapidly gained currency from the 1960s on.

Our family may have been Americans, and proud of our Irish heritage and close familial ties there, but above all, we were Catholics. As such, it was very hard for us collectively to stomach the divergence between what leading Democrats, including Senator Edward Kennedy, said about abortion (to name one topic) and what our Church teaches us. As a young, practising Catholic, it enraged me. And upon discovering what Republicans – Pat Buchanan was one whose speeches during his insurgent 1992 primary challenge to President George HW Bush and regular media contributions I found compelling – had to say, I gravitated to the GOP and joined the party shortly after my 18th birthday. This was my version of teenage rebellion. Sad but true.

Notwithstanding his own grievances with the mother ship, Dad deemed this an act of both unfathomable apostasy and colossal stupidity, given our family history and my desire to continue it. The path to a career in elected politics for a Republican in Massachusetts was then, and remains today, an exceedingly narrow one. When his family discovered my political identity, either when it was whispered or became manifest in the arguments I tended to deliberately instigate, they muttered to themselves or solemnly shook their heads. At any rate, it put paid to any notions I might have otherwise had about catapulting onto the scene. So I started at the bottom: trying to get elected to the non-partisan town meeting.

The New England Town Meeting has its origins in the 17th century. Puritans who went to the American colonies to pursue religious freedom wanted to have a forum in which to discuss and decide upon community-specific matters. In its purest form, the town meeting allows all citizens to directly deliberate and vote on legislation. An eminent Massachusetts historian calls it 'the most democratic form of government one can imagine. It's the closest to the people; it involves the largest number of people; it's the most open.'[2]

Although it may sound odd to say, such an open system, in which all citizens have a vote, is arguably the easiest to manipulate and hence subject to criticism for being undemocratic in the context of a small town. Historically, wealthy and educated people could mobilise those of the same social class, and intimidate those whose livelihoods depended upon them, to attend the often lengthy proceedings and dictate what was decided in public votes, whether it was in the best interests of the majority of a town's residents or not.

For that reason, and because of the inherent tendency of open town meetings to be unwieldy, many towns across New England have adopted representative town meetings in which the members are elected. The Boston-abutting town where I grew up, Milton, Massachusetts, is one such municipality. The town meeting members still have to keep their ears to the ground in that there are 279 members, elected in ten precincts (small electoral areas), who serve Milton's roughly 27,000 residents. That's one town meeting member for every 97 citizens. It may not be direct democracy, but it's reasonably close to it.

Milton itself was once a town known for being where wealthy and prosperous Protestants decamped to from Boston's tony, but cramped, Beacon Hill and Back Bay sections to inhabit large, stately homes with salubrious surrounds to match. By way of example, the aforementioned first President Bush was born in one of these mansions, at the top of Milton Hill looking across Boston Harbour toward the city skyline.

2 Charlotte Lubov, 'Town Meetings: History in Action', *New York Times*, 6 May 1990 (quoting Charles Collier).

Situated just seven miles from the bustling downtown and bordering the city's Dorchester, Hyde Park and Mattapan neighbourhoods, Milton offers a perfect blend of easy access by both private and public transit to workplaces, educational institutions and amenities together with a less frenetic suburban lifestyle.

Slowly but surely, many Boston Irish settled there, displaced most of their Brahmin predecessors and assumed the town's political leadership. Until very recently, it was the 'most Irish' city or town in the United States and is still near the top of a list which is dominated by Boston suburbs. In particular, the less well-to-do East Milton, my home neighbourhood, was 'taken over' (to quote the less-than-complimentary greeting offered by one long-time resident to a friend's father) from the 1950s onward by first- and second-generation Irish-Americans who had gained entry to the professions, as well as by Irish-born men and women who had succeeded in a variety of trades. At least half of my friends' parents were Irish emigrants, the overwhelming majority of whom hailed from Galway. Ireland and Irishness were inescapable in East Milton and constituted a core element of our shared identity. For instance, there may have been nods to religious and secular holidays at St Agatha School, which many of us attended. But St. Patrick's Day was set aside for a lengthy programme of events during class time featuring Irish dancing, music and food. Jerseys touting our hometown – or close-by towns and city neighbourhoods – usually bore shamrocks. Even in a multicultural society, it did not seem at all out of place, such was the prevalence of Irishness in our lives.

It was in the midst of this perhaps over-idealised milieu, then, that I set off looking for signatures to secure a place on the ballot for the first time. And did I ever get an education in practical politics that Harvard's Kennedy School of Government couldn't deliver.

The first door I knocked on was answered by a neighbour from an old Milton Protestant family who I knew in passing. Knees knocking and teeth chattering, I blurted out why I was there and what I was looking for. Whether it was with a snarl or a good-natured smirk I'll never know, because my head was down in fear, he snatched the clipboard, scribbled his name and said something like: 'I shoulda known you'd get in this game … you just better not raise my taxes if you get in.' Elated with this success at the first door, I moved on.

I spent the entire afternoon at it. Some houses were empty; others were clearly occupied but my knocks and doorbell rings were ignored. The reactions from those who were good enough to open the doors ran the gamut. Several elderly people commented that it was nice to see a young person take an interest in the community and not only signed my nomination papers, but pledged to vote for me on polling day. On the other hand, one clearly stressed middle-aged man offered a harsh, yet fair in hindsight, series of observations and declined to sign the papers after sizing me up and listening to my well-rehearsed spiel: 'You're a full-time student with no clue what the real world is like; you live with your parents who still take care of you; you don't have a mortgage; you don't pay taxes; you don't have the pressure of raising a family; you can't represent me.'

Even though my father had prepared me for attacks, and my assumption was that the poor guy was having a bad day, it was still sobering and tough to take. But all these years later, his are the only words that I can repeat verbatim. From the moment I meekly and dejectedly walked down his front porch steps, the platitudes I had always mouthed about respecting anyone with the guts to put his or her neck on the line and invite the judgement of others became real in a very new way.

Having people willing to do so is the bedrock of our democracies. And that's why I have so little time and patience for those who reflexively are critical, or even loathing, of politicians. Of course, there are some whose motives are less than pure and a small minority who are downright malevolent. In this vein, however, politicians, as a whole, are only a reflection of us all.

That day, I managed to garner approximately 50 signatures. My father had urged that I get double the required 25 in order to account for people who might not be registered to vote or who lived outside the precinct, but would sign nonetheless. Thankfully, upon returning the official documents to the town clerk's office, more than 25 were certified and my spot on the ballot was guaranteed. I drafted a press release – in hindsight, it was too long and too boastful – that was printed in the local newspapers, and photocopied hundreds of half-page fliers saying: 'ELECT LAWRENCE P. DONNELLY – TOWN MEETING MEMBER – PRECINCT 6.' My father and I pushed them through the letter boxes of registered voters in our neighbourhood. I also attended pre-election forums and showed up anywhere else voters were likely to be in decent numbers. In those days, before social media, that was about all I could do. The response to my candidacy was generally positive – notwithstanding the persistent, disbelieving murmurs about my being a Republican. Because Milton town elections are non-partisan, it was not a disqualifying offence for most voters. Were it for a seat in the state legislature, it most likely would have been.

All that was left was preparing for the date of the election and ensuring that my family, friends and neighbours remembered that I was on the ballot and that I needed their help to win. Perhaps paradoxically, these types of elections, even though they have the most significant and tangible impacts on the citizens of a city or town in many ways, invariably engender the least amount of interest and lowest rate of participation. Most average Americans are busy with work and family and don't have the time or inclination to read local news or engage with local issues. State, federal and national campaigns attract so much traditional and social media attention that they are hard to avoid and hence attract higher (though still low by international comparison) rates of participation. This is a pity, especially in that some could contribute significantly to their communities.

Despite the widespread apathy, we did the best we could and awaited the results to come in on local access cable television. And when all the votes had been counted, I was duly elected. I did not come first, but ran closer to the top than the bottom of the cadre of men and women who prevailed. Crucially, I was competing with a number of well-known incumbents and was among the strongest finishers of those elected for the first time.

'Not bad,' was my father's understated reaction. My mother, as ever, was far more impressed.

It was a nice feeling to have won, albeit at the very ground floor. My law studies and other realities of life kicked in before I would represent Precinct 6 at the annual town meeting the following week. Still, it was an enjoyable evening that I look back on fondly to this day. I remember saying to my dad that it could offer a platform to run for something else. Knowingly, he replied that such a bid would be futile unless I changed parties or undertook a run in order to be rewarded with a government job in return for offering myself up as a sacrificial lamb. Nonetheless, as the ambitious dreamer I undeniably was, I couldn't help but wonder if it marked the start of something big. Given my family history, it was only natural that I might get carried away with this political success. It was something we were fairly accustomed to.

Part One – The Boston Family Business

CHAPTER I

The Kelly Brothers

The Boston neighbourhood of Dorchester was founded as its own separate town in the early to mid 17th century by Puritans who had emigrated from Dorchester, Dorset, England. Dorchester was annexed by the city in 1870 and is, by a long stretch, the largest neighbourhood in Boston, which happens to be among the smallest of America's urban centres in geographic terms. Not unusually, it was originally inhabited by a Native American tribe from the Massachusett nation, the Neponset, and the river dividing Dorchester from suburban Milton is named for them.

It was well served by rail from downtown and had thus become a very popular countryside getaway for the Boston elite in the 19th century. Notwithstanding its distinctly English roots, however, Dorchester became a place where many European immigrants, those from Ireland in particular, settled in the early 20th century. They were joined in increasing numbers by black Americans fleeing hostile territory in the southern US, as well as by immigrants from Africa, Asia and the Caribbean. Today, that ethnic mix – together with an influx of people from around the country who have come to

Boston for higher education or for work or for both – renders Dorchester a uniquely diverse and vibrant place to live.

Near the turn of the 20th century, my own family from the west of Ireland – from north County Galway on my paternal grandmother's side and from Kiltoom, near Athlone, in County Roscommon on my paternal grandfather's – arrived in Dorchester and found tens of thousands of fellow Irish emigrants already in full pursuit of their American dreams. They, and those from other European countries, carried with them a strong Catholic faith. As such, Dorchester had a number of thronged churches.

Indeed, Dorchester people, both those who remain and those who have left but revere their roots in the old neighbourhood, identify themselves to this very day by which Catholic parish their family hails from. My family settled first in St. Peter's Parish, in the northern part of the neighbourhood near Meetinghouse Hill, the highest point in Dorchester.

One native, the painter Childe Hassam, lyrically summed up the reasons why the area was so attractive to newcomers:

> Dorchester was a most beautiful and pleasant place for a boy to grow up and go to school – from Meetinghouse Hill and Milton Hill looking out on Dorchester Bay and Boston Harbour with the white sails and the blue water of our clear and radiant North American weather ... if you like as fair as the isles of Greece ... and white houses often of very simple and good architecture juxtaposed to it all. Some of the white churches were actual masterpieces of architecture, and the white church on Meetinghouse Hill as I look back on it was no exception.

Boston then was dominated by prosperous families who collectively ran the city and controlled its financial, cultural and other key institutions. They were largely white Anglo-Saxon Protestants who, in some cases, were downright hostile or condescending toward the mainly Catholic immigrants suddenly in their midst. In that context, the new Bostonians made their way as best they could in the public and private sectors. In light of their rapidly growing numbers, politics was one route that ethnic Catholic immigrants saw toward a better life for themselves and for those from their respective tribes. And it was there that my great-uncles, Frank and John Kelly, directed their energies and ambitions.

In countless and endless chats in the vicinity of the Massachusetts State House on Beacon Hill, Frank Kelly was remembered by a good friend of mine, the late, consummate political animal and public servant, Don Falvey, as 'one of the all-time characters in Boston politics'. Frank was a relatively newly qualified attorney when first elected to the Boston City Council in 1929 at age 26. While on the council, the young upstart jousted frequently with one of the most legendary Irish-American politicians in history, James Michael Curley.

What more can be said about Curley, the son of Galway-born parents who served as a state legislator, a US Congressman, for four terms as Mayor of Boston and for one term as Governor of Massachusetts over half a century in public life, that hasn't already been chronicled in the history books or biographies? Curley was convicted twice of serious offences – the first of which was taking a civil service exam for an Irish immigrant who could not read or write. He parlayed that into a subsequent successful election slogan: 'he did it for a friend'.

Later on, in 1932, he was denied a slot as a delegate to the Democratic National Convention by a political foe. Undaunted, he assumed an alias, Jaime Miguel Curleo, and was selected as a delegate from Puerto Rico! At some stage prior to or during Curley's governorship in the 1930s, a tenure described as 'ludicrous part of the time, shocking most of the time, and tawdry all the time', he offered to nominate his erstwhile foe on the city council, Frank Kelly, to take up a coveted position on the quintessential bastion of the Boston legal establishment, the Supreme Judicial Court of Massachusetts, if and when a vacancy arose. Although my Uncle Frank may have been tempted by the chance to horrify the genteel, Ivy League scholars on the oldest appellate court in America, elective office was where his heart lay. Accordingly, 'Stick it where the sun doesn't shine' was his curt response to Governor Curley's entreaty.

After his service on the Boston City Council, Uncle Frank (as he was known in our house) sought to be elected lieutenant governor of his state in 1936. Triumphant in the Democratic primary, he faced off against the then-Speaker of the Massachusetts House of Representatives, Leverett Saltonstall. 'Salty' was an aristocrat who could trace his family genealogy back to the *Mayflower*, the ship that carried the first Pilgrims from England to Plymouth Plantation in 1620. A graduate of Harvard University and Harvard Law School, he was a veteran of World War I. He was equally a political figure straight from central casting for that era and the ideal foil for Frank Kelly.

From the off, Uncle Frank painted him as a rich Yankee, totally out of touch with the various challenges faced by ordinary people, especially the working-class Irish in Boston and across smaller cities and towns in Massachusetts. He also had a typically Brahmin name, Leverett being borne by several in his family before him and likely the converted surname of another ancestor. In short, 'Leverett Saltonstall' said everything: the name itself was an emblem of his exalted socio-economic status. To it, at a campaign debate, Frank Kelly added the middle initial 'P' to devastating effect. He intoned, in a broad Boston accent, 'my opponent, Leverett Percival Saltonstall' at the outset.

Contriving an even more esoteric and noble middle name for his Republican opponent was a stroke of political genius insofar as it drew the class distinction between the two men into sharp contrast: Leverett Percival Saltonstall vs Frank Kelly. Uncle Frank won that race by a mere 7,000 votes from well over a million that were cast. It was the only time Saltonstall, who went on to be Governor and US Senator from Massachusetts, was ever defeated in a state-wide election. He never forgot it. My father recalls being present for an unexpected meeting of the two by-then elderly men, who maintained a lifelong friendly relationship, in the mid 1970s on State Street in downtown Boston. On recognising his old rival, Saltonstall exclaimed, 'Goddamn you, Francis, they are still calling me Leverett P!'

Returning to the 1930s, Frank's brother John won election to the Boston City Council in his own right representing Ward 15 and St. Peter's Parish in 1937. In 1946, with the assistance of Mayor Curley, John Kelly became President of the Boston

City Council. The plot then thickened. John was indicted on a charge of soliciting bribes in April of 1947, but was fully acquitted that June. Almost immediately after his acquittal, however, Mayor Curley was sentenced to prison for mail fraud. The city charter provided that John Kelly would serve as acting mayor for as long as Curley was away. But this was a bridge way too far for Boston's WASPish establishment.

In *Building a New Boston: Politics and Urban Renewal, 1950–1970*, the Boston College historian Thomas O'Connor writes: 'The acting council president at that moment was John B. Kelly, brother of Francis E. Kelly ... the prospect of the Kelly brothers running the city of Boston did not at all appeal to the downtown Republicans, and at that point Governor Robert F. Bradford moved into the vacuum and arranged for the state legislature to appoint the Boston city clerk as acting mayor.'[3] Naturally, John was bitterly disappointed. And to add insult to injury, following a campaign in which he adopted a slogan that alluded directly to his legal travails – 'Re-Elect John B. Kelly: Proven Honest' – he was defeated in his bid for re-election to the city council. That marked the end of his career in politics.

His brother Frank, on the other hand, furthered his career in law and in elective office. He successfully ran for Attorney General of Massachusetts in 1948 and won a second, two-year term in 1950. 1952, though, was a good year for the Republican Party and Frank lost his bid for a third term.

It is worth noting that one Massachusetts Democrat who bucked the trend that November was John F. Kennedy. The

---

3   Thomas O'Connor, *Building a New Boston: Politics and Urban Renewal 1950–1970* (Northeastern University Press, 1995).

Republican presidential nominee, Dwight Eisenhower, won the state by more than 200,000 votes. Yet Kennedy managed to beat his GOP foe for a US senate seat, Henry Cabot Lodge, by some 70,000. Frank Kelly was not the only Democrat sharing the state-wide ticket with the future president who wondered if he was already looking past the rough and tumble of Massachusetts politics to the White House.

And speaking of rough and tumble, the former Boston City Councillor, historian and author, Larry DiCara, recounts a 'dispute' between Frank Kelly and a local reporter on the campaign trail in 1952. After a debate with the Republican nominee, George Fingold, Frank was asked by a reporter about rumours that he held substantial amounts of money of unknown, dodgy origin in accounts in banks throughout Boston. Frank's reaction was to slug the reporter in the face; unfortunately for him, the incident was captured by a press photographer. Even more unfortunately for him, DiCara was told a quarter of a century on by a Republican operative that he had witnessed the punch first hand and purchased the photo for $100, a handsome sum in those days, and Fingold used it to devastating effect in the campaign's closing days.

As well as serving in and pursuing public office, Frank Kelly built a hugely successful law practice. He specialised in representing plaintiffs who had suffered personal injuries and was involved in the early days of the Massachusetts Academy of Trial Attorneys. A cynic might term him an ambulance chaser, but by all accounts he was a very capable advocate for people with little experience of the court system and who would have otherwise been denied access to justice had he not intervened. My own mother, who worked as a legal secretary in a prominent insurance defence firm, used to describe the way her bosses would react when they were to do battle against Frank Kelly closer to the end of his legal career, and wonders what they might have said if they didn't know she was dating his nephew. One technique he employed frequently when up against WASPish, 'white shoe' law firms defending Boston's entrenched financial interests was to flick a set of rosary beads from his pocket while purportedly reaching for his handkerchief. Juries in eastern Massachusetts, predominantly Irish and Catholic in those days, lapped it up. 'You could almost hear the cash register opening, cha-ching, cha-ching,' an old-timer once told me.

Frank Kelly's lucrative law practice – coupled to a lesser extent with, as Larry DiCara describes, then-extremely loose campaign finance laws which did not forbid serial candidates for political office like Frank from raising money and having a substantial income, yet no salary – made him a wealthy man. It was entirely permissible to run for office often, collect funds and live on them. No doubt reflecting the mores of that period, my father would often tell the story of his elderly Uncle Frank lamenting the practices of the next generation of Massachusetts politicians on a commuter boat from his second home in the town of Hull, situated across Boston Harbour from the city.

'These kids today, Larry,' he muttered while looking disdainfully into the distance.

'What is it, Uncle Frank?'

'They take cheques,' was his disgusted response.

Those who react to the story in horror would do well to

consider that typically ethnic Catholic Boston Democrats had almost no connections to the corridors of real money and power. Their Republican opponents were invariably either from extremely wealthy families or were 'sponsored' by an establishment that clung steadfastly to their standing at the top and resented new immigrants and others who challenged them.

Frank had settled with his family in a large house on Morton Street in St. Gregory's Parish in Dorchester. St. Gregory's, as compared to his native St. Peter's, was a lace curtain, even well-to-do area. And Larry DiCara calls this fairly affluent section of Dorchester a political powerhouse during his childhood. 'You had Mayor John Hynes, Attorney General Edward McCormack, State Treasurer John Driscoll, Frank Kelly and a host of other local politicians within a few streets of one another – it was the political capital of Massachusetts.' And indeed, St. Gregory's bred future politicians, DiCara and Brian Donnelly among them. Mayor Hynes, the son of a Galway immigrant, was one of Boston's modernising mayors. McCormack is most famous for his unsuccessful campaign for US Senate in 1962 against a young Edward Kennedy. During a debate, McCormack memorably roared at his privileged opponent, 'If your name was Edward Moore and not Edward Moore Kennedy, your candidacy would be a joke.'

Frank Kelly's political last hurrah came that same year. He decided to run again for Attorney General. Leading Massachusetts Democrats had other ideas and endorsed a much younger state legislator, James Lawton, for the position at the party convention. The Kennedy–McCormack match-up was box office stuff, attracted extraordinary media attention and drove turnout way up. Uncle Frank, having been a well-known state-wide official and political figure for decades, benefitted hugely from his name being far better recognised by casual voters and pulled off a major upset in the primary. The Republican nominee, Edward Brooke, who later became a US Senator, was an African-American.

Frank Kelly was a master of running against Boston's Protestant ruling class; he had no idea how to run against a black man. In his previous tenure as Attorney General, he was a strident advocate for civil rights and for equality. But pressure mounted from some of his long-time contributors and backers to exploit the issue of race. There were elements, acting on their own and without the approval of the campaign, who engaged in despicable behaviour. In *From Edward Brooke to Barack Obama: African American Political Success, 1966–2008*, Dennis Nordin outlines the use by 'forces supportive of Kelly' of the n-word and other outrageous tactics to scare white people into voting for their man.[4] And in an undeniable misstep, Frank also referred directly to Brooke's race in the middle of a debate. While some historians have drawn negative inferences about Frank Kelly as a consequence, those who knew the man never thought he was a racist and he is broadly looked back upon with fondness. Nonetheless, it was a regrettable end. Perhaps Uncle Frank's most lasting legacy was the creation of the Massachusetts State Lottery, a crucial vehicle for funding local government expenditure, an initiative he championed relentlessly.

4   Dennis S. Nordin, *From Edward Brooke to Barack Obama: African American Political Success, 1966–2008* (University of Missouri Press, 2012).

The controversial Tory MP Enoch Powell said that all political careers end in failure. If the low point of Frank Kelly's political career was playing the race card in 1962, it highlighted just how potent race was, and remains, in American life.

CHAPTER 2

A Changing Boston

A little over a decade after Frank Kelly's political career
reached its denouement, in September of 1974,
parents of school-aged children in Boston were
gripped by fear as to what might lie ahead.

The civil rights movement and the resistance to it in the
American South that boiled over in the 1960s was, of course,
watched with a mixture of curiosity and shame in the northeast.
Most Bostonians, however, felt that the activism and bigotry
simultaneously on display was other-worldly. That said, it
all came to their city in 1974. Parents' annual late summer
routines had been rendered infinitely more complicated and
fraught by a ruling from federal judge W. Arthur Garrity that
the city's public schools were racially imbalanced. That finding
was undeniably correct. But the remedy Judge Garrity chose
to desegregate the schools was more controversial. He ordered
students to be bused across the city, i.e., white students from
mainly white neighbourhoods would have to attend schools in
predominantly black neighbourhoods and vice versa.

Put simply, many Boston public school students could no
longer walk to the school they lived across the street or down
the road from. Instead, they were forced to board at least one

bus and embark upon a journey to a different, maybe far-flung part of the city. This was despite the fact that their parents might have attended the same school themselves and bought or rented a home so that their children could have the same educational experience they did. And these children had to get on a bus and face a far longer and more turbulent school day through absolutely no fault whatsoever of theirs or their parents.

These facts are unassailable. Yet as ever, there is more to it than that. Judge Garrity was a native of Worcester, Massachusetts, a city some 40 miles away from Boston, and a graduate of the College of the Holy Cross (my own alma mater) and Harvard Law School who went on to be a dependable aide to John F. Kennedy in his 1960 presidential campaign and was subsequently appointed a federal judge. As J. Anthony Lukas writes in *Common Ground: A Turbulent Decade in the Lives of Three American Families*, Judge Garrity was part of a cadre of second- and third-generation Irish-Americans who had found 'homes in the suburbs', were 'making their way in law, medicine or business' and were 'too assimilated to enjoy the raucous, boozy and sometimes violent celebration [of St. Patrick's Day] in South Boston'.[5]

His critics allege that it was a consequent combination of ignorance, indifference and condescension with respect to the working-class Boston Irish that animated his thought processes in devising a plan for forced busing. Indeed, the plan implemented by the judge in 1974 and thereafter impacted most heavily upon two largely Irish-American neighbourhoods:

5   J. Anthony Lukas, *Common Ground: A Turbulent Decade in the Lives of Three American Families* (Vintage Books, 1985).

South Boston and Charlestown. The Italian American neighbourhood of East Boston, home to Logan International Airport and connected to the rest of the city by a tunnel under Boston Harbor, was left untouched, while the picturesque streets of the Italian North End, adjacent to the city centre, received only a small influx of Asian American students from nearby Chinatown.

It was signalled to Judge Garrity and to city politicians by organised crime figures and others that the tunnel would be the site of mass protests or even blown up if buses were sent through it en route to schools in East Boston. Given the airport's location, this could have had a crippling effect on the local economy. Whatever the credibility of the threats, East Boston's isolated geography eventually ruled it out of the plan. Moreover, the potential for a truly metropolitan solution never seems to have featured on any collective radar screen. Boston, by American standards, is a tiny city geographically. There seems to have been no good reason why surrounding, then virtually all-white, suburban communities with outstanding school systems could not have been incorporated into the plan. Some have cited a United States Supreme Court precedent that would have militated against a broader solution, yet these were exceptional, distinguishable circumstances in Boston. That the suburbs were spared and that Judge Garrity resided in one of the most affluent of them provided plenty of fodder for city politicians who vehemently opposed busing and who appealed to the Boston families most affected by it.

These families lived in neighbourhoods like South Boston, Charlestown and my family's stomping grounds, Dorchester.

They were defined by the core values of hard work, civic mindedness and generosity. Irishness featured prominently as well, and still does, albeit to a lesser extent, today. For many who originally hailed from there and prospered economically, the lure of the suburbs – larger homes, big back yards, less urban noise and hustle and bustle, better schools – prevailed and they moved out. Others, however, were committed to staying. Busing changed that for a significant portion of that cohort. Once Judge Garrity decreed that their children couldn't, as of right, attend the school nearest to where they lived, many parents who could afford to do so fled. Those who had no choice stayed and did the best they could.

The Donnellys were among those committed to city living. My father was fiercely loyal to the place that he thought was a slice of heaven on Earth: the Lower Mills section of Dorchester. Had it not been for forced busing and all the upheaval that accompanied it, he – and, in turn, we – *never* would have left it. The Milton I grew up in was chock-full of 'busing refugees': Bostonians who felt like they had to go elsewhere, yet wanted to stay as close as possible to where they had originated. The house I was raised in is slightly more than two miles from Clearwater Drive, where my father spent his formative years. In the busing era, though, the unaffected town of Milton, which is a separate municipality and school district, was a world removed from the tumult unfolding right next door.

Dad never warmed to Milton. Tales about him and his friends being followed by the town's police after they crossed over the city line from Dorchester and snarls that his two sons were 'helpless Milton kids' when we misbehaved were common in our childhood. It may have been a mere half-hour walk away at a brisk pace, but I will eternally wonder at how fundamentally different our lives would have been if we'd stayed in Boston proper. There are tens of thousands in the same shoes as us. Many of them never contemplated it – mainly because they and their parents desperately wanted to put busing behind them. But as someone whose father never allowed what he called 'an evil perpetrated on innocent people by a rotten human being [Judge Garrity]' to be forgotten, busing was always there for me. More broadly, we will never know what Boston might be like today if it weren't for the mass exodus equally engendered and accelerated by the judge's order.

In the years prior to 1974, Boston was rapidly diversifying. The African-American population in the city's Roxbury and Mattapan sections, as well as parts of Dorchester, expanded enormously in that time. Sadly, city politicians, especially the then elected members of the school committee, did not welcome these newcomers and instead pandered to the fears of city residents about them. One aspect of this was the neglect of schools in these areas. Typically, black boys and girls went to public schools in buildings that were crumbling and often poorly staffed. Their educational experience and attainment paled by comparison to those of white students in the city as a result. And the school committee did not move swiftly enough to redress matters, even when pushed by forces in the city and well beyond its boundaries. That school committee was comprised of several politicians who played to their constituents' worst instincts and uttered racist epithets themselves.

In the end, these self-interested politicians actually betrayed the Bostonians they claimed to want to protect. For if they hadn't been so recalcitrant and had provided the badly needed resources to schools attended by African Americans in a city that was changing and diversifying inevitably, the draconian solution of forced busing possibly could have been avoided. Additionally, it is worth pointing out Boston's evolution as a city of ethnic neighbourhoods. The city may have been segregated racially, but it was also segregated ethnically. Dorchester, South Boston and Charlestown celebrated their Irish heritage; East Boston and the North End revelled in their Italian roots. The neighbourhoods acquired their ethnic character as immigrants settled and wanted to retain a piece of the old world in a new country. If the school committee engaged constructively in this vein, things may have played out very differently and more satisfactorily from their own vantage point. Instead, they played lowest-common-denominator politics in front of a constituency that was afraid and didn't know where else to turn. There is no denying that some of the men and women who elected candidates with disturbing and hateful views shared those sentiments.

Yet on the other hand, many likely saw these politicians as the only ones who would look out for them and for their interests at a time when money and power were flowing out of city neighbourhoods. A host of influential observers, locally and nationally, reached the same conclusion about these Boston residents: they were racists and deserved whatever they got. Their assessment is manifest in the media coverage throughout the busing crisis. What it overlooks, though, is that these working-class people only wanted the same thing that the cognoscenti who judged Boston's parents so harshly had already obtained for their own children: the best education possible. When pushed, outsiders could not say that they thought it would be good for their own children to be forced to get on a bus and travel away from a school in their own locality. Anti-busing activists rallied around politicians who recognised that injustice. Some initially thought Senator Edward Kennedy, from a storied political clan with a commendable track record of fighting for the marginalised and vulnerable, would see it and help figure out a better way forward. The senator had actually indicated on more than one previous occasion that he opposed the forced busing of students to achieve school desegregation. But the anti-busers were wrong.

The main citizens' organisation established to fight the implementation of busing in Boston was known as ROAR (Restore Our Alienated Rights). ROAR planned massive demonstrations in the city just prior to the start of the school year in 1974. The group had invited Senator Kennedy to its prior gatherings, but he had declined to turn up. On the eve of this one, however, *Boston Globe* columnist Mike Barnicle wrote a piece called 'An Open Letter to Senator Kennedy'. In it, he employed these rousing words:

Tomorrow, they'll be marching ... people who have worked hard to stay even, never mind get ahead. Many of their minds can still race back in time and history to the night that 'one of their own,' John Fitzgerald Kennedy, became the President of the United States of America. That was an earlier, easier time for them, a time when it was easy to smile and laugh. But there will be few smiles tomorrow and little laughter ... Senator, you are the one man who can heal the divisions that have arisen over the issue of busing. You have the one voice that can help keep this city calm, leaving the clear ring of justice and common sense ... You could recall your memories of your brother, Bob, being driven through the streets of Gary, Indiana, with hands reaching out to touch him, hands that came out of a gray factory dusk and touched him in a night of brotherhood, hands – black and white – that were alive with hope. You could tell them, Senator, that law knows no neighbourhood, that justice is not confined to any one block, that fear must be put aside and the fact of law adhered to. And to you, Senator Kennedy, they would listen.[6]

Of the three Kennedy brothers who served in elective office, Edward (hereinafter Ted) was the least likely politician. From the beginning, his capacity was questioned and many observers didn't think he had anywhere near the 'fire in the belly' for the toughest business of them all. History ultimately proved his critics were far off the mark. But back then, he was, naturally, shattered by the assassinations of his two older brothers and damaged in myriad ways by the drowning of Mary Jo Kopechne after the car he was driving, in which she was a passenger, plunged off a bridge on Chappaquiddick Island near Martha's Vineyard in 1969. As he continued to try and put that awful incident behind him, politically and otherwise, busing was a crisis that Ted Kennedy did not need.

6   Mike Barnicle, 'An Open Letter to Senator Kennedy', *Boston Globe*, 8 September 1974.

Whether he read Mike Barnicle's column or not, he did go to the ROAR rally the following day. Almost immediately after arriving at it, Senator Kennedy had to know that he had made a huge mistake. He was jeered incessantly.

'Impeach him. Get rid of the bum.'

'You're a disgrace to the Irish!'

'Let your daughter get bused, so she can get raped!'

'Why don't you let them shoot you, like they shot your brother?'

'Kill him!'

He was shouted down when he took a microphone and attempted to address the thousands gathered there. He reluctantly left the podium and, surrounded by police, strode toward the nearby federal building named after his brother. Members of the crowd advanced toward him, throwing tomatoes, eggs and other projectiles in his direction. News bulletins uniformly announced that a Kennedy had never been greeted with such hostility on home turf.[7] From 1974 onward, though, these Bostonians harboured an intense personal dislike for Ted Kennedy that bordered on the vicious.

In those years, the city often did resemble a 'war zone', as one mother memorably put it in a television interview at the time in a very strong Boston accent. The September 9 surge against Senator Kennedy was only the tip of the iceberg. In one iconic photo that won a Pulitzer Prize, a white teenager was depicted as assaulting a black attorney and architect, Ted Landsmark, with a flagpole that had the American flag affixed to it. There were anti-busing demonstrations with

7 J. Anthony Lukas, *Common Ground: A Turbulent Decade in the Lives of Three American Families* (Vintage Books, 1985).

angry hordes of men and women of all ages protesting, getting into skirmishes with police in full riot gear, hurling objects at buses, law enforcement officials and black schoolchildren and yelling racial epithets laden with obscenities. When it became clear that peaceful protests would not stop the buses from dropping students at schools, some ridiculed the tactics of the mainstream anti-busing movement and agitated for violence.

It was sentiment like this that most worried the woman who was the *de facto* leader of the anti-busing movement, Louise Day Hicks of South Boston. The daughter of a judge, Mrs Hicks became a lawyer herself and served in elective office for much of the 1960s and 1970s. She started off as a liberal, but her popularity skyrocketed when she opted to become the face of resistance to pressure from within and without to undertake proactive measures to desegregate the school system. Her campaign slogan – 'you know where I stand' – allowed voters to read into it whatever they wished, and more often than not, what they feared. Her critics alleged it was a 'bigot's code'.

She and her supporters were lampooned in the national media, most offensively in an arguably anti-Irish 1967 *Newsweek* magazine story on her quest to become mayor.

> They looked like characters out of Moon Mullins, and she was their hometown Mamie made good. Sloshing beer at the long tables in the unadorned room of the South Boston Social and Athletic Club sat a comic-strip gallery of tipplers and brawlers and their tinselled, overdressed dolls ... After Mrs. Hicks had finished off reading off her familiar recitation of civic wrongs the other night ... the men queued up to give Louise their best, unscrewing cigar

butts from their chins to buss her noisily on the cheek, or pumping her arm as if it were a jack handle under a trailer truck.[8]

Like any good politician, Mrs Hicks sought to use it to her benefit. In a responsive full-page newspaper ad, she said: 'I deeply resent your insults to Boston and its residents ... I am proud of my heritage. No article of yours can lessen that pride.'[9]

So much of Mrs Hicks' political appeal flowed from her persona and her refusal to apologise for who she was. 'Boston for the Bostonians' was another of her rallying cries and it was an intentional rebuke to 'do gooders' and outsiders. But as a lawyer herself and the daughter of a judge, she had a stronger understanding of the rule of law than most in the anti-busing movement. She also rejected the more violent and anarchic *modus operandi* which radicals in ROAR and the groups that splintered off the organisation favoured. She typically urged conflict avoidance and was attacked by some allies for doing so. Another of her slogans was that she was the 'only mother on the ballot' and, in her single term in the US House of Representatives, she was an advocate for the equal rights amendment. Mrs Hicks also was a champion of organised labour who claimed to have never crossed a picket line in her life.

Herein lies another perhaps surprising truth about the political fallout from forced busing. Irish-Americans and other Bostonians who vehemently opposed busing did not gravitate in significant numbers to the Republican Party. Most were

8   Ibid.
9   Ibid.

Democrats through and through. As much as they despaired at what those who they admired, Senator Ted Kennedy foremost among them, had done, they did not leave what had always been their home. Instead, at local level, they stayed within the tent and fought with the progressives who they believed (not without justification) disdained them. They argued that the party should avoid social engineering and stick to basics. This provided the backdrop for many fierce primary contests throughout the 1970s, 1980s and 1990s between what emerged as two factions of Massachusetts Democrats. And even as the more conservative wing backed Ronald Reagan for president, they clung to the label that they were 'Reagan Democrats' and their mantra was that 'we didn't leave our party; our party left us'. A similar dynamic took root within the party across the US.

Elsewhere, though, the flight to the GOP was sure and swift. This may be because those disenchanted Democrats, most of whom immigrated to the US much earlier than those in eastern Massachusetts, weren't as aware either of what their party had done for them or how hostile Republicans had been.

Ultimately, as the years and buses continued to roll by, the war against busing subsided and Bostonians got on with their lives as best they could. The damage was considerable, however. The compelling personal stories of both black and white students in Boston in the mid-1970s paint a terrible picture. Many white students, who were often encouraged to boycott school, either dropped out without obtaining a high school diploma or just about scraped by and never made it to college. Black students, far from getting the superior education busing was intended to deliver, were subjected to racist taunts on a daily basis and had to try to learn in an environment where security trumped pedagogy. There was a litany of racially motivated, violent incidents. A high percentage of Bostonians who could afford to leave the city did so. The crucial middle class was diminished. I have never heard anyone argue credibly that it worked well. In fact, it is a lot easier to make the case that it was a total disaster, a failed experiment in which black and white students and their parents without economic means were unwitting pawns. There was a similar dynamic in other American cities and it was surprising to hear Kamala Harris, who was herself bused, make Joe Biden's opposition to what had largely failed a campaign issue as they sought the Democratic presidential nomination in 2019 and 2020.

I have serious misgivings about the racism that undeniably animated elements of the anti-busing movement in Boston. But in my view, fear and desperation were the most prominent emotions felt by the majority. They weren't all haters. Fear and desperation united them. They fought busing with everything they had. They fought the system and the outsiders who controlled the system. Those outsiders included Judge Garrity, the *Boston Globe* and, yes, Senator Ted Kennedy. It was a fight they couldn't win. Yet they still fought to the end. In their conduct of this doomed struggle, the former President of the Massachusetts State Senate and of the University of Massachusetts, South Boston's William Bulger, once appropriately said: 'They were courageous. They were steadfast. And they were right.'

I was not born when Judge Garrity made his decision. I was a toddler in the mid-1970s when Boston was brought to its knees. But the impact of busing on my political conscience was profound and lasting. I am instinctively distrustful and wary of liberal elitists who always assume they know best and make policy accordingly. This superior attitude was what was most galling about busing advocates. All too often, those who have taken up similar causes don't have to live with their dictates; other people do and, when they object, they are labelled or condescended to. There has always been an element of this within the Democratic Party in the US, and it is manifest in the European left, too, especially when it comes to the 'culture wars'.

As such, while I may today be a proud Democrat who takes issue with so much of the philosophy that has historically underpinned the Republican Party, no one would confuse me with a leftist. In fact, had I ever been elected to the US Congress or the state legislature, I probably would have found it just as trying to do business with the liberals in my own party as with unwavering right-wingers on the other side of the aisle. I suspect that neither was easy for my Uncle Brian in Boston or in Washington. And yet, it is in both of these complex arenas that the former high school teacher and coach made his mark.

CHAPTER 3

Brian Donnelly:
A Politician Is Born

From his beachfront home on Cape Cod, reflecting on a 26-year political career that uniquely made him more of a household name in a country 3,000 miles away than in his own, Brian Donnelly believes that Boston politicians have been blamed somewhat unfairly for their alleged intransigence in the run-up to the busing crisis. 'There was definitely a mix of good and bad on the school committee. Yet people like Kevin White [Mayor of Boston during the 1970s], Larry DiCara and others did their best under awful circumstances.' As a first-term member of the Massachusetts House of Representatives, he attended a meeting in the early 1970s on the closing of a small and much beloved school in Dorchester. He believes it was a turning point.

That school was being shuttered because the school committee, in order to facilitate the desegregation of the city's education system, was building larger, modern schools on the rough boundary lines between mainly white and predominantly black areas. Parents, however, furiously opposed its closure. They exerted enough pressure that a member of the school committee changed his vote and the school was preserved. Then, as my uncle puts it, 'all hell broke loose' and 'the road was paved for Garrity to design and implement his disastrous, mean-spirited solution'. As he says, 'it was a horrible, horrible time for everybody in the city'.

Brian was raised by my grandparents, Larry and Pauline, from Roscommon and Galway emigrant families respectively, on Clearwater Drive in St. Gregory's Parish in the Lower Mills section of Dorchester. Larry, the first in a line of four of us to bear the name, was a civil and structural engineer for the Commonwealth of Massachusetts while Pauline stayed at home to raise their four kids. My dad was the eldest, followed by Louise, Paul and Brian, the youngest. Louise became a registered nurse who worked in a variety of care settings at the same time as being a devoted mother to six children. Paul qualified as a mechanical engineer and an architect, and subsequently went into academia, ultimately holding a professorship and an endowed chair in the School of Architecture at Washington University in St. Louis, Missouri. He still works as an architect now for the city of Boston in a senior position, first hired for his expertise by Mayor Martin J. Walsh. Dad qualified as an attorney, and later was appointed to serve as a state and federal administrative law judge. Brian went into the family business.

Brian graduated from Catholic Memorial High School and then from Boston University, where he majored in physical education. He became a teacher in the Boston school system and worked at schools in Dorchester, Roxbury and the North End. Given that his uncles had both been prominent politicians and that he was civically engaged, it came as no real surprise when he decided to run for one of three seats in the state legislature in 1972 from Dorchester's 12th Suffolk District. As city residents were leaving for the suburbs, Brian was very active in the movement to convince his fellow Dorchesterites (colloquially known as 'Dot Rats') to stay there – that it was their community and they should fight to preserve all that made it such a wonderful place to live.

In the politically active neighbourhood, there were more than 20 candidates in the outsized field. One journalist posited that the ballot paper 'looked like the Dublin phonebook', such was the dominance of Irish surnames. As was customary in those days, it became a battle among Dorchester's Catholic parishes for supremacy. There were fewer candidates from St. Gregory's than from the others and this worked to Brian's advantage. The most prominent was a former state representative, Bill Keenan, who was a highly decorated World War II veteran and of an older generation. My father remembers that voters found Brian's charismatic personality and youthful energy very persuasive and opted to give a younger man a chance.

On a lighter note, he also recalls an endorsement from Frank Kelly for his nephew. Cards posted out to neighbours and supporters featured a large smiling photo of Uncle Frank, a list of his own accomplishments, a caption in huge capital letters describing him as 'ONE OF DORCHESTER'S HIGHEST EVER ELECTED OFFICIALS' and, finally, a one-line request in small print asking that they vote for Brian Donnelly for state representative! This may have helped, too. At any rate, Brian was one of the three runners elected.

One day, shortly after he took office, he brought my grandmother to the State House with him. As they strolled down the corridor, Brian said hello to a police officer charged with providing security to members of the legislature. 'Hi Pat!'

To his astonishment, my grandmother looked at the very same man and said, not overly warmly: 'Hello Bernard.'

Stunned, Brian asked, 'How the hell do you know Captain Murphy from Galway, and why are you calling him Bernard?'

My grandmother replied, 'He's your cousin.' It turns out that my grandmother's first cousin had also emigrated and built a good life for himself – and, indeed, was using a different first name – in Massachusetts. In a not uncommon occurrence, particularly in Irish-American families, some distance had grown up between them. In the years to come, that distance would be diminished immeasurably.

But back then, the fresh-faced legislator was only finding his feet when the number of state representatives was cut from 240 to 160. In a power play designed to keep their own seats safe, other Dorchester lawmakers pushed Brian out of parts of their own constituency and into the most left-leaning, still WASPish precinct in Milton and into the heavily Italian American Hyde Park section of Boston. My father would always say: 'They intended to destroy Brian Donnelly, politically speaking. Instead, they created a monster.' Brian did just fine with the old Yankees on Milton Hill; Brian made Hyde Park his own with the assistance of an aide to State Senator Joe Timilty, also from Dorchester Lower Mills, with whom he had become friendly when they helped lead Timilty's close-run campaign for Mayor of Boston in 1975.

That aide was Hyde Park's own Tom Menino, who went on many years later to break the Irish stranglehold on the mayoralty and serve for two decades in City Hall before he passed away in 2014. Menino brought Brian around Hyde Park and introduced him glowingly to the numerous large Italian families whose votes and backing were vital. They warmed to Brian quickly, rallied around him and he kept his seat against the odds. This was significant insofar as it showed that he could appeal to men and women from outside his own Dorchester Irish tribe. His thoughts and ambitions, unsurprisingly, turned from Boston and the State House on Beacon Hill toward Washington, DC and Capitol Hill.

Brian resided in what was then the 11th Massachusetts Congressional District. Oft-gerrymandered, the 11th was represented previously by such luminaries as John Quincy Adams (notably after he had served a term as President of the United States), John F. Kennedy and Tip O'Neill. Rumours abounded in the mid-1970s that the district's long-time incumbent, Democrat James Burke, was slowing down. In 1976, a California transplant with a good name for the heavily Irish district, Patrick McCarthy, decided to challenge Burke in the primary. He fell short, yet performed reasonably well and achieved a good deal of notoriety and favourable media coverage in the process. The Speaker of the US House of Representatives, Tip O'Neill, was among those impressed by McCarthy. At the same time, though, he alienated Burke's core backers who resented the 'carpetbagger' who nearly dislodged their man. Before Burke announced whether he would seek another term in the 1978 election, Brian Donnelly declared his candidacy for the Democratic nomination. More than 40 years on, Brian believes emphatically that his ultimate victory in that race was down to two key ingredients: 'being the right person in the right place at the right time' and 'third-party endorsements'.

Burke decided to bow out. That left four strong candidates: Brian Donnelly, Pat McCarthy, Patrick McDonough, a Boston City Councillor, and James Sheets, a well-regarded politician with a strong base in the city of Quincy, just south of Boston. McCarthy and Brian were quickly acknowledged to be the frontrunners. They were both Irish-Americans, but the similarities ended there.

McCarthy was a strident leftist who enjoyed the backing of advocates for far-reaching campaign finance and related reforms in Washington in the wake of the Watergate scandal and of activists for liberal abortion laws. Brian was an old-fashioned, 'bread and butter' Democrat whose progressive outlook on economic issues and social conservatism reflected his Catholic upbringing. McCarthy's campaign headquarters was a swanky, business-like environment. Brian had eight offices in various places around the district and was reported to have 'overwhelmed' its cities and town with the most lawn signs and bumper stickers touting his candidacy by a long stretch. While McCarthy was prone to dwell on policy details to bolster his profile, the *Boston Globe* noted that a simultaneously simple and effective television ad had Brian 'in a supermarket, carrying a bag of groceries for a sweet old lady'.

In that newspaper, Mike Barnicle both encapsulated the stark distinction between the two men and sagely forecast how the election would pan out:

Jobs, and food prices, and pumping oil into the spigot alongside the house, and the modest yard dominate the thinking of the electorate. A handshake and a promise to be back mean more than 40 position papers on the situation in Rhodesia.

And when you've used the years to take the family out to the suburbs and invest in the house with the lawn, you're looking hard at someone like Brian Donnelly, who sounds as angry as most of the voters feel. It could be that Pat McCarthy is just too polite.[10]

The 11th congressional district in 1978 comprised three principal areas: first, the Boston neighbourhoods of Dorchester and Hyde Park where the people knew Brian well and had elected him to the state legislature overwhelmingly; second, Quincy and close-in Boston suburbs, such as Milton and Braintree, which were then, and remain today, chock-full of families originally from Dorchester; third, the working-class city of Brockton 25 miles to the south and further out towns like Stoughton and Randolph. The first two areas were relatively straightforward in the sense that they were tailor-made for Brian. Moreover, as a popular state legislator, he had the backing of most of his influential elected colleagues who represented these cities, towns and neighbourhoods. The last was more complicated.

The towns of Randolph (where Pat McCarthy lived) and Stoughton, especially the former, had sizable Jewish populations. Brian was fortunate in that he had grown up in Lower Mills,

10 Mike Barnicle, 'Latest line on race in 11th District', *Boston Globe*, 14 September 1978.

which bordered the formerly heavily Jewish neighbourhood of Mattapan, and had attended the Taylor School as a boy in Dorchester, where many of his classmates were Jewish. When Jewish families left the city for the suburbs, lots of them went to Randolph and Stoughton. On the campaign trail there, he had something important in common with many contemporaries and their families who similarly cherished their days at the Taylor School.

Brockton was a rather different kettle of fish and was then a heavily Italian American city. It was known nationally for two things: it was a place where shoes were manufactured and where the boxing legend, Rocky Marciano, hailed from. In the late 1970s, shoe manufacturing had slowed and the city was down on its luck. Marciano was the heavyweight champion of the world in the 1950s and had died tragically in a plane crash in the Midwestern US in 1969. His extraordinary career and premature death made him a godlike figure in the city. To this day, Brockton is known as the 'city of champions' owing to Marciano's storied career in the ring and its subsequent favourite fighting son, Marvin Hagler. For Brian Donnelly from Dorchester, this was most unfamiliar territory.

At the outset, he had three angles to win over initially sceptical Brockton voters. First, he was close to the legislative delegation from the city and they were supportive of him. Second, he had demonstrated an affinity with Italian voters in Hyde Park and, as a result, was keenly aware of the cultural differences between them and the Irish. Third, in one Brockton ward, there was a substantial constituency of residents who had migrated down from Dorchester and instinctively thought of Brian as one of them. The old neighbourhood's tentacles were everywhere.

These were all fruitful. But Brian also benefitted crucially from a major unforced error committed by Pat McCarthy. In fairness to him, McCarthy recognised that shoe manufacturing was largely gone and not coming back and, while the city was right to take pride in its native son Marciano, that wasn't going to put food on the table for struggling families. He had a comprehensive plan to transform Brockton into a hub for burgeoning high-technology firms and related businesses. It was actually quite visionary in some respects. Its unveiling, however, was an absolutely devastating train wreck. McCarthy sunk himself with one loud proclamation: 'The days of shoes and Marciano are over!'

The reaction in Brockton was dismal, to put it mildly. Many retirees who had spent their entire working lives in shoe factories and bought homes and raised families with their hard-earned wages were both horrified and offended by an apparently cavalier dismissal of what had meant so much to them. At the same time, the disrespect afforded to their fighting idol, a symbol of the city's resilience in the face of adversity, went down like a lead balloon. Brian benefitted immensely. Rocky Marciano's elderly and hugely admired mother, Pasqualina, a native of Campania in Italy, immediately got in contact. She offered an enthusiastic endorsement and assumed the honorary title of chairwoman of Brian's campaign. Fast-forwarding four decades, with a chuckle at his unexpected luck and newfound ally back then, he says that 'we put her name on literally everything down there'.

Just before the primary was to be held, perhaps sensing the direction the wind was blowing, the retiring Congressman Burke informed the media that he would be supporting Brian Donnelly. With that strong breeze fully at his back that Tuesday, 14 September 1978, Brian cruised to a comprehensive victory across the district and became his party's nominee to serve in the 96th United States Congress. Given that the district was so heavily Democratic, this was the *de facto* election. It was, according to my father, a fantastic night of celebrations and an extraordinary moment above all for my grandmother who was there to take it all in. And even talking about it years later, my father's pride in his younger brother's accomplishment was always palpable.

In the days after the election, Brian, in addition to spending some time with his wife, my Aunt Ginny, travelled down to Washington, DC to meet with the Speaker of the House, Tip O'Neill, and other prominent members of the Democratic leadership. Although it may have been slightly awkward on the surface, in that Speaker O'Neill was known to have favoured another candidate in the race, there were no grudges and it was quickly put behind the two men. They formed a mutually beneficial friendship. Additionally, Brian made a strong impression on others in the leadership of the House of Representatives that would, in time, ensure his rise in influence.

Brian also called into another friend of his, President Jimmy Carter. The Carter campaign had employed a unique strategy of deploying its urban supporters to other cities in 1976. Accordingly, Brian and a cadre of Boston politicians (my father also accompanied them) went to Philadelphia and did the things that they knew best to drive high turnout, manage expectations, reconcile competing factions, etc.: the nuts and bolts of urban ethnic politics. This crew from Boston helped Carter win the battleground state of Pennsylvania over President Gerald Ford and the man from Georgia was grateful.

A signed picture of their one-on-one meeting in the Oval Office hangs on the wall of the sitting room of the house I grew up in to this very day. It reads: 'Best wishes to my good friend, Brian Donnelly.' As Brian himself said in his boisterous election-night address to an elated crowd of family, friends and supporters, 'Not bad for a 32-year-old kid from Dorchester whose family came over in a boat.' Not bad, indeed. I only wish I was old enough at the time to have fully grasped and appreciated it.

CHAPTER 4

A Congressman Who Loathed the Limelight

The Washington, DC that Brian Donnelly arrived in was still in many ways dominated by the aftermath of the Vietnam War and by the Watergate scandal, in which President Richard Nixon sought to cover up a break-in at the headquarters of the Democratic National Committee in the Watergate office building, and subsequent impeachment hearings which resulted in Nixon's resignation. Beforehand, Congress had been a genteel, even clubby environment, but Watergate focused new attention on the role of money in American politics and engendered a widespread clamour for reform.

The 96th United States Congress, which convened from early 1979 to early 1981, was Brian's first. Both the Senate and the House of Representatives were controlled by the Democrats who had considerable majorities. They held 58 of 100 seats in the upper chamber and began the term with 276 seats, compared to 156 for the Republicans, in the House. But the Democratic Party was a far more ideologically diverse and less cohesive entity in those days.

Brian recalls that the 'leadership had to live and lead by consensus. You had the urban ethnic Catholics like me – mainly from the northeast, but also from other pockets in big cities around the country; you had the southern Democrats; and increasingly, you had the more doctrinaire liberals who run the show on Capitol Hill now. The liberals were still in the minority when I first got there.'

Brian asserts that, because the three rough groupings represented very different constituencies, they had very different priorities and political antennae.

> My crowd were very concerned about ours becoming the party of the elite. Most of us were Irish or Italian (or both) in terms of our family backgrounds. There were also some Germans, Polish and French-Canadians in the mix. For us, it was 'We are the party of ordinary working people and let's not ever take our eye off that ball.' Some of the liberals thought we were relics whose outlook was well beyond its sell by date. They may have won the war ultimately. Looking at the state of play today, though, we were right.

The southern Democrats, in his view, have been assessed and treated too harshly by pundits and political scientists. Notwithstanding the fact that many southerners gravitated toward the Republican Party at national level because they did not approve of civil rights legislation, they often voted for Democrats to represent them in the US House of Representatives or in the state legislature owing to their personal appeal or to their espousing more centrist or nuanced stances on the issues that mattered most to them. They were collectively known as southern Democrats. Brian says:

> The smart ones among them knew back then which way the game was headed, that they were an endangered species. And those who now allege that they were all racists and haters have got it wrong. Sure, a handful of them were. But the way that their districts were drawn up then, they needed to get every black vote they possibly could, together with a minority of the white vote. Whites in the south were moving to the GOP swiftly. Because of the votes they needed to win, most of the southern Democrats I dealt with were moderates, but distinguishable from what the media now says are moderates. They were very progressive on economics and religious conservatives. That was the winning formula for them.

On the other hand, the liberals were driven and determined to move the party in their direction. There was a multitude of politicians who fell into this category and came to prominence in the 1970s and 1980s. The present Speaker of the House, Nancy Pelosi, who was first elected to represent San Francisco in 1986, may be the best known. The party has transformed so utterly since that Pelosi herself is now seen as an establishment-oriented and centrist-leaning Democrat in 2021. Of these politicians, Brian believes:

> A lot of them derived their political consciousness from opposition to the Vietnam War or revulsion at the Watergate scandal. They wanted us to move way left on abortion and other cultural issues and they pushed hard for

reforms. They were very sceptical, and in many instances repelled by, some of the leadership in both the House and the Senate and they wanted to take over. To an extent, I admired their zeal, but I thought that they were unfair to some of the old-timers, who really believed in our party's ideals and took a lot of risks to put them on the statute books. I also think their political calculus was off – that we would alienate millions of our people with this kind of high-minded, trendy, left-wing advocacy. I still do. The reason we had control of the House for so long was because we zeroed in on economic, bread-and-butter issues that we knew most Americans were with us on. I don't know if the liberals didn't believe that or recognised it and didn't care – or what. To me, it was just plain dumb politics.

In short, he says, 'You can see how Tip [O'Neill, the Speaker of the House from 1977 to 1987] had a really tough job to keep everyone happy and on board. I think he did it really well under complex and trying circumstances. There were lots of times when I didn't envy him.'

For a variety of reasons, the US Congress Brian served in for 14 years was a wholly unrecognisable institution when contrasted with what exists in 2021. On the other side of the aisle, the GOP leadership stood much, much closer to the centre than it does today. It was long before the Newt Gingrich-led 'Republican Revolution' took advantage of widespread voter apathy and dissatisfaction in 1994 and brought dozens of hard-right conservatives to Capitol Hill. Some are still there today; others have been succeeded by even more fervent right-wing activists.

There was no internet or social media. C-SPAN, the network which televises many congressional proceedings, was in its infancy. And maybe above all, CNN had also just been founded and there were no biased and partisan cable news networks rooted in and perpetually exacerbating political hyper-polarisation, such as Fox News and MSNBC. Many who served alongside Brian say that it was a nice, friendly and relaxed place where ideological foes could still collaborate and act in the country's best interest – at least sometimes. President Ronald Reagan and Tip O'Neill occasionally getting together for a drink is but one legendary example of a time in American politics that has been consigned to the history books and whose extinction is widely lamented.

This climate was as conducive to Brian Donnelly's rising up the ranks as the composition of his district was to his election. In what will come as a profound shock to contemporary observers of politics, Brian was well known for doggedly and assiduously avoiding publicity and keeping as low a profile as possible. He didn't want his name in the paper or his face on TV. Instead, he preferred working behind the scenes to advance the causes he believed in most deeply and the interests of his constituents back in eastern Massachusetts.

Thanks in large part to a push by Speaker O'Neill, Brian won a coveted spot on the powerful House Ways and Means Committee. The committee's principal responsibilities are for reviewing and making budget expenditure recommendations and for the US tax code. As one colleague, the late Congressman Joe Moakley from South Boston, put it shortly after Brian had left Congress, 'He took to it like a duck to water.' Indeed, the dollars and cents were what mattered most to the old-fashioned Boston politician.

As Brian said to me of a Democratic contemporary in the House who took a different view and preferred to be on the Judiciary Committee: 'He must have been out of his mind. Do you think the average people in Quincy or Brockton who voted for me and who I was down there to fight for gave a damn about constitutional law?' This comment in fact sums up why Ways and Means was the place for him. Gifted with a charismatic personality and a manner that was at the same time easy-going and blunt, he was among its most effective members. His common-sense approach garnered first the respect and thereafter the friendship of the long-time Ways and Means chair, Dan Rostenkowski, a fellow urban ethnic Catholic from Chicago.

One of the projects that consumed a huge amount of his time and energy on Ways and Means was the mammoth Tax Reform Act of 1986, which was intended to simplify the tax code. On the one hand, it lowered the highest tax rate; on the other, it eliminated many of the tax deductions and shelters that wealthy people, together with their accountants, utilised to limit the amount of money they paid over annually to the Internal Revenue Service. It was President Reagan's number-one domestic priority in his second term in the White House and was touted by his allies as the single biggest reform of the tax system in the nation's history. While praising the noble sentiments that animated it and ensured that an overwhelming bi-partisan coalition of members of Congress enshrined it into law, Brian had major difficulties with what happened in the timeframe from the introduction of the initial bill to its being signed by the president.

The bill was the subject of fierce lobbying by an array of influential vested interests who objected to sections or, indeed, the totality of the far-reaching legislation. The grubby tug of war and the relationships between lobbyists, many of whom were former members of the House or the Senate, and politicians was even the subject of a best-selling book, *Showdown at Gucci Gulch*. Brian was one of the key players during the negotiations over the bill and became disenchanted. After all the wrangling, because what was originally put forward had become so watered down, he 'barely voted for it in the end' and regards the purported reform as a 'failure'. He found working on a Ways and Means subcommittee trying to bring the costs of healthcare under control a similarly frustrating task.

At any rate, by the mid-1980s, Brian was established as a low-key, yet well-respected, member of the House who was close to the top Democrats. One of those was another Irish-American, Tom Foley, from the state of Washington. Foley had been in Congress since the mid-1960s and served in a variety of leadership posts. When the speakership became vacant following an ethics investigation into the Texan Democrat, Jim Wright, Foley sought to replace him. Owing to their friendship and aware of how personally popular Brian was with their colleagues, Foley tapped him to run his campaign for the post. And he won it easily.

In those years, however, Brian became slowly frustrated by life in Washington, DC, and in Congress. On the one hand, his party continued to move leftward culturally. On the other, driven, he says 'first by the California delegation [including Nancy Pelosi] because of how expensive it was to win a campaign there and then by the New Yorkers who wanted Wall Street money', the elected officials moved away from its core constituency of 'lunch bucket Democrats'. As the party realigned, it became a colder place for Democrats of Brian Donnelly's hue. Moreover, with a wife and two young children back in Boston, the weekly commute of almost 500 miles each way and the countless hours spent on planes and in airports began to grate and Brian started to think about life after Congress, even though his seat was as safe as safe can be. In early 1992 then, he took many Massachusetts political observers by total surprise when he announced that he would not seek re-election to an eighth term.

The previous year, he had been approached by the up-and-coming and avowedly centrist Governor of Arkansas, Bill Clinton, who was seeking his support as he prepared to mount a campaign for the Democratic nomination to take on President George HW Bush. Clinton was aware that Paul Tsongas – a former US Senator from Massachusetts who was one of his main rivals for the nomination – and Brian were not close. And Clinton strategically desired the potential endorsement from a fellow politician from the same state. Because of his moderate messaging, then Governor Clinton was a natural choice for Brian. It might not have been an exact quid pro quo, but having promised his backing, Brian expressed a strong interest in becoming the US Ambassador to Ireland. Clinton was receptive.

It was not to be, however. Ted Kennedy was still among the most powerful members of the US Senate, and would be pivotal to Bill and Hillary Clinton's promised healthcare reform. As the most well-known Irish-American in the country, he would not take kindly to the Kennedys being passed over for such an eminent posting by a politician from their home state. Furthermore, Hillary Clinton objected strenuously to Brian's long record of votes opposing liberal abortion legislation. For these reasons and possibly other political considerations, Brian was passed over for the job he really wanted and Jean Kennedy Smith was nominated to take up residence in the Phoenix Park.

My family took it hard. To this day, I can't forget my father exploding in rage when the political journalist Eleanor Clift, who was thought to be friendly with Mrs Clinton, predicted in March 1993 on *The McLaughlin Group* (then a very popular weekend political TV programme) that 'Jean Kennedy Smith, not the rumoured favourite Brian Donnelly, will be the Clinton administration's Ambassador to Ireland'. The House Speaker, Tom Foley, was not pleased either. In fairness to Kennedy Smith, however, she did acquit herself well and exceeded the expectations many set for her in her tenure in Dublin.

1993 presented another tantalising political opportunity for Brian, though. Boston Mayor Ray Flynn, who had served in office for a decade, was appointed US Ambassador to the Vatican by President Clinton. Flynn was succeeded as interim mayor by Brian's old friend and emissary to Italian Americans earlier in his political career, Tom Menino. As a resident of Boston's most populous neighbourhood, an Irish-American and an ex-Congressman, Brian became, as one observer wrote, 'the 750-pound gorilla' about to get in the ring. It was a pretty clear reference to the three-quarters of a million dollars that still lay in his political campaign account. He would have been a formidable candidate.

Yet it would have been a very tough fight in a city that had changed inexorably since he first ran for state representative. Many of the old families had left for the suburbs or retirement in Florida and there were far more people of colour, whose backing Menino had spent years as a city councillor cultivating unremittingly. In my father's view, the luck and timing so necessary to win a political campaign would not be with him and he argued that Brian should give it a miss. The city was too different and Menino was too well-ensconced as interim mayor. Looking back on it, Brian's old friend, Larry DiCara, agrees that Tom Menino would not have been beaten. Despite being urged to get in by a wide cross-section of Bostonians, Brian made the difficult decision not to enter the race. Menino was elected easily over an Irish-American state representative from Dorchester, Jim Brett.

From my own point of view, 1992 and 1993 were when I fully grasped how prominent my godfather, with whom I shared a surname, was. There was tremendous media attention on Brian's abrupt departure from a safe congressional seat, the rumours that he would become US Ambassador to Ireland and then on his possibly seeking the mayoralty of Boston. He was all over the newspapers, the radio and the television. I was taking full notice for the first time. I was intoxicated by the speculation about him and the related questions I was fielding from near and far – none of which I had anything remotely resembling the answers to! It was during this period that, in many such encounters, I got a sense of all that my Uncle Brian had done to help people and how grateful they were to him for it. It made me realise that politics is a noble profession and that I absolutely had to be involved somehow in it.

Naturally, I had known that he had been a congressman for as long as I could remember and greatly enjoyed the family trips we took to Washington, DC and the VIP treatment we often got. I got used to the fact that we had neighbours who would make a point of coming to our house for a drink or two on Thanksgiving when they knew he would be there and could later tell others that they had enjoyed their congressman's company. And even as a young boy I could recognise the magnetism that he possessed in spades – how quite literally everyone in every room he was in gravitated to him and never walked away with anything but a smile on their faces and a certainty that he was a 'regular guy' who had spoken to them with the same good nature and inquisitiveness as he would speak to the president. Even allowing for my undeniable bias, my uncle was a truly gifted politician.

In the end, Brian did make a significant contribution as an American diplomat. First, he worked alongside the US Ambassador to the United Nations, Madeleine Albright, as the US Representative to the UN General Assembly, which he described as an 'extraordinary experience'. He was then nominated by President Clinton and confirmed by the US Senate as US Ambassador to the Caribbean nation of Trinidad and Tobago. He was praised by locals and US foreign service officials alike for his performance. In a 1995 *Boston Globe* profile, entitled 'Mr Ambassador', the head of the country's chamber of commerce commented: 'We need all the help we can get, and I think Brian Donnelly will be there to help us. If anyone can address them, Brian Donnelly can. Brian lives, breathes, drinks politics. Politicians speak a special language. He may be more Republican than Democrat.'[11]

That profile closed with an inevitable question. Will you go back into politics? He responded frankly: 'I could. I love the thrill of the battle. People may have forgotten about me … But I'm going home. And home is Massachusetts.' Indeed, there was one more campaign in Brian, an unsuccessful run for the Democratic nomination for governor in 1998. It was the only race he ever lost. He had been away for a while; he was deemed by many on the left a figure of a past they no longer approved of; some old enemies from the media were lying in wait for him. Massachusetts Democrats had become more liberal and Brian's opposition to abortion, for example, was something they could not accept. That said, many of the wiser old heads in the party believed that the man the progressives favoured, Attorney General Scott Harshbarger, was too far out of the mainstream and that Brian would be a much better foe for the popular Italian American Republican nominee, Paul Cellucci. They were right in that Cellucci won the governorship, but their admonitions went unheeded as Brian stumbled to a distant third-place finish in the Democratic primary. Nonetheless, his was a remarkable career in public life. And one of the very unusual things about it was that Brian Donnelly became far more well known and celebrated in another country, his ancestral Ireland, than he was in the country where he was actually elected.

11 Brian McGrory, 'Mr Ambassador', *Boston Globe*, 29 January 1995.

CHAPTER 5

Ireland's Man in Washington, DC

B rian Donnelly recalls being told by countless people in his constituency that Ireland was an economic basket case in the 1980s. Speaking to me in 2020, former Taoiseach Bertie Ahern puts some flesh on just how hard things were.

> Unemployment was hovering around 20 per cent and youth employment was between 50 and 60 per cent. It was horrendous for families in that period; it was just shocking stuff. To put it starkly, there are 2.4 million people working in Ireland today, but back then, there were less than one million working. There were loads of young men and women going to America illegally. We are very lucky that Brian Donnelly was there when Ireland needed him.

Brian's 11th congressional district had the heaviest concentration of people of Irish descent and, by a significant margin, the highest number of Irish-born men and women in the US. There was a steady stream of contact from constituents desperately seeking his assistance for younger relations who were living in the shadows of America as 'illegal aliens' or were stuck in Ireland, often highly educated, yet unable to obtain employment. On one steamy summer day, two elderly Irish gentlemen waited for hours outside his office in Quincy before being summoned in so that they could tell their families' stories. Brian was moved by their plight. At the same time, the Irish Immigration Reform Movement (IIRM), a grassroots movement of Irish and Irish-American advocates, sprang up. It was led by, among others, a young emigrant from County Louth who went on to become a well-known author and the founder of the *Irish Voice* newspaper and of IrishCentral.com, Niall O'Dowd.

O'Dowd says that the IIRM was started by two young Cork men, Seán Minihane and Pat Hurley. They met at their home county's club in the Queens borough of New York City to discuss the plight of young men and women coming illegally to the US. They decided to call a public meeting and hundreds of undocumented Irish showed up. O'Dowd believes that Minihane, in particular, was a natural leader. One of the problems this new generation kept coming up against was older Irish emigrants who kept saying that the young Irish should 'keep their heads down and make no waves'.

O'Dowd was very aggressive in combatting that sentiment – as was Minihane. O'Dowd says that he founded his newspaper, the *Irish Voice*, in 1987 'precisely because so many were fleeing home for a new life in America at the time and there was a need for a youth-oriented community newspaper'. Its first headline – We're Never Going Back – was deliberately provocative and based on a survey of the undocumented who overwhelmingly told *Irish Voice* journalists that the US was their new home and they were ready to fight for it. The effort to legalise the Irish was greatly helped by the billionaire philanthropist Chuck Feeney (with whom O'Dowd was close), who provided critical funding for the lobbying effort.

O'Dowd and others in the IIRM soon discovered that they had a staunch ally in Washington in Brian Donnelly. As O'Dowd puts it, 'Brian was the 1980s version of Richie Neal [current Congressman and Chair of the Congressional Friends of Ireland]. He was the go-to guy for everything Irish with a deep and sincere interest in helping people of all backgrounds, but especially the Irish.' Of course, our family's background made him instinctively sympathetic, but the ethnic composition of his district meant that being proactive on this front could yield political dividends as well. Brian and his staff turned to the last major piece of legislation on the topic, the 1965 Immigration Act.

That Act, which was spearheaded by Senator Edward Kennedy among others, was intended to allow more people from developing countries to come to the US and had family reunification as one of its core objectives. One of its unintended consequences, however, was to discriminate against putative immigrants from Europe. Ireland, because of its long history of emigration, was particularly adversely affected. Even Congressman Peter Rodino, who wrote the 1965 Bill, did not foresee this disproportionate impact and, when made fully aware of it by Brian, asked him: 'How do we fix this?' As the son of an Italian immigrant from humble origins and a liberal fixture on Capitol Hill since the 1940s, Rodino regretted his lack of foresight and was a great asset to ameliorating things for the Irish.

They struck upon the idea of a diversity visa lottery system which still exists today. And this became known – at least for the Irish – as the Donnelly Visa. A 2017 *New York Times* article chronicling its origins characterised it as follows:

> The program had its origins in the Immigration Act of 1965, which eliminated country quotas that had favored Western Europeans and replaced them with an immigration system based mainly on family reunification. After the 1965 law went into effect, immigration from Asia and Latin America soared but arrivals from Ireland, Italy and other European countries dropped precipitously. In the 1980s, Irish-American congressmen led by Brian Donnelly, a Democrat from Boston, drafted a temporary measure, which passed in 1986. It provided an alternative path to a green card for citizens of countries adversely affected by the 1965 reforms, including Ireland.[12]

There was an awful lot of hard work and political machinations that went on behind the scenes to get the Donnelly Visa over the line. There was no significant opposition within Congress, but it is a difficult place to get anything done. And immigration is a vexed issue that most politicians approach with an abundance of caution. Republicans are inclined to oppose permissive proposals. Democrats, even then, would have been conscious of the fast-growing Latino population and wary of doing something special for the Irish. The Irish government was equally careful in its approach – conscious both that being too demanding could alienate American leaders and that more

12 Miriam Jordan, 'Diversity Visa Lottery: Inside the Program That Admitted a Terror Suspect', *New York Times*, 1 November 2017.

visas could accelerate a 'brain drain' of the country's best and brightest who would be essential to future prosperity at home.

Niall O'Dowd notes that Brendan Scannell, an Irish diplomat then based in Boston, was hugely important in quietly persuading the Irish government to come onside. Back in Dublin, the government, for all sorts of reasons, was wary of getting fully behind this initiative. O'Dowd believes that Scannell's work and close collaboration with Donnelly's congressional staff was crucial. There was still animosity at the time in some influential Irish-American quarters over how the Irish government had handled the Troubles, but Scannell and Donnelly brought the stakeholders to the table and ensured they worked in concert.

O'Dowd describes both Speaker Tip O'Neill and Senator Kennedy as:

> huge players who were very sympathetic. But it was always tense and it was Donnelly who was the prime mover. He was exceptionally close to O'Neill who gave him the green light in framing the legislation. The IIRM activists proved themselves charming and persuasive lobbyists and, at Donnelly's urging, approached every major member of the House from both parties. His colleague from Boston, Congressman Joe Moakley also helped on a couple of key instances when there were procedural delays. And with his enormous clout, Senator Kennedy cleared the way in the upper chamber. As a grassroots movement, the IIRM was extraordinary. There were literally thousands of people at their rallies. Politicians took note.

Due to the IIRM's newfound political power and Donnelly's adroit manoeuvring, 40% of the visas in the diversity lottery were ultimately set aside for Irish applicants. I'll never forget the mass meetings explaining how to apply for the visas and the stories of 'Donnelly Visa parties' here in the US and back at home. When the visas were eventually awarded, Ireland got the bulk of the 40,000 available. It surpassed our wildest dreams at the time.

In the midst of all this, O'Dowd recalls some good times, too, and how he got to know and like Brian as a friend.

One of my lasting memories is a freezing January night in Queens and making my way in awful conditions to an IIRM fundraiser where the special guest was Brian Donnelly. I just wasn't sure how many people would turn up to listen to this guy from Boston. I need not have worried. There were over 1,000 people there. They lined up and waited to meet him. Many were in tears and couldn't thank him enough for allowing them to stay in a new country they had made their own. He was visibly moved, but he downplayed the praise. All he would say was 'That's why I'm in politics … to help people.'

He also recounts a raucous mid-March celebration one year in Manhattan for which they stayed out until the wee hours. Niall O'Dowd says he 'woke up in a midtown hotel room with no recollection of how I got there. Meanwhile, Brian arrived at the airport in plenty of time for a 7 a.m. flight to Savannah, Georgia, where he was the Grand Marshall of their massive St. Patrick's Day Parade. I still don't know how he made it!'

Brian was a frequent visitor to Galway and took a strong interest in building upon the close familial ties between the west of Ireland and the Boston area. The former Galway West TD, Irish government minister and European Commissioner, Máire Geoghegan-Quinn, first encountered him at a clinic for constituents in the city. 'The clinic was being held in Richardson's, a pub in Eyre Square. And in walked Brian Donnelly. Loads of women in Galway were mad about him – and I don't think he was even aware of it.' It was no surprise that Brian walked into Richardson's, as cousins of ours, the O'Loughlins, had a shop just a couple of doors down.

Geoghegan-Quinn has always had close familial ties to the US. Uncles and aunts had emigrated there, and her son lives in the southern US today with his American-born wife and son. She terms the Donnelly Visa a trailblazer for many people from her native Connemara. Her friends and neighbours were in constant contact with her about their sons and daughters who were desperate to travel the well-trodden path of their predecessors who had made the sound of the Irish language being spoken not at all uncommon in Dorchester, South Boston, Milton and Quincy – places many of them actually knew better than Dublin. Geoghegan-Quinn's perception was that it was Brian's likeability that helped the Donnelly Visa overcome the labyrinthine impediments to almost all proposed legislation in Washington, DC. 'People would stop him in Galway and talk to him because they would recognise him. He was always affable and friendly, yet there was a certain shyness in him – not the usual brashness that people from the west of Ireland would associate with Americans. They loved him.'

Her most tangible realisation of what the Donnelly Visa meant to the people who elected her to Dáil Éireann faithfully for decades came closer to the end of her time in elective office. She travelled to Boston in 1994 at the request of the Taoiseach at the time, Albert Reynolds, to attend the funeral of Tip O'Neill. She spent much of her time with Brian and the then Irish Ambassador to the US, Dermot Gallagher. Having dinner in Anthony's Pier Four restaurant on Boston Harbour, she overheard a couple having a flowing conversation in Connemara Irish. No doubt curious and ever the politician, she had to ask where they were from and how long they had been in what many Galway people still refer to as the next parish over. 'We got Donnelly Visas,' was their immediate response. Geoghegan-Quinn says that 'Brian had been away from the table and returned to a heartfelt greeting from a man and woman who were Connemara people, just like me, yet had become American thanks to him. It was wonderful to be able to introduce them.'

Geoghegan-Quinn states firmly that his Irish background was not something he played up because it was trendy or politically helpful. 'You'd almost say that he was born and reared in Ireland, such was his commitment to our issues.' Geoghegan-Quinn is a staunch advocate for gender equality. And she partly attributes Brian's desire to assist the Irish and others who were struggling to the story he once told her about my grandmother. After he had been elected to Congress, Brian took his mother to the Ritz-Carlton, an elite Boston hotel, for dinner. But she steadfastly refused to enter after she had been chauffeured there, pointing out that she remembered two signs that once hung outside: 'No Irish' and 'No dogs'. 'That's where his conscience was formed,' she believes.

That conscience, which made him so loyal to his ancestral country, extended his attention and energies well beyond the problem of youth unemployment and emigration. As the Irish government sought to realise the vision of people like the Taoiseach in the first part of the 1960s, Seán Lemass, and the eminent civil servant, TK Whitaker, and attract inward investment from the US, Bertie Ahern says that he was 'immensely helpful' in terms of opening doors and cultivating influential contacts for him and his colleagues throughout the 1980s. Those meetings helped to create the International Financial Services Centre, to raise a new consciousness that Ireland was an ideally situated location for American multinationals to base themselves in Europe and to plant the seeds for the transformative Celtic Tiger economic boom.

And, of course, Northern Ireland and the Troubles were high on the agenda for Irish-Americans at that time. It may have come as a surprise to some, yet Brian was deeply sceptical of the Irish Republican Army and the provisional movement. My father claims that this attitude was instinctive; like many Irish families, ours had a long history of service and a consequent respect for the British Army. Several members of my dad's father's family – hailing from close to Athlone where there was a major British Army installation – were highly decorated British Army veterans. To what extent his family background shaped his perspective is unknowable, but Brian did not buy into some of the fables that circulated in Irish-America about the republican movement and abhorred the outlandish rhetoric that often flowed from barstools in neighbourhood bars in Irish strongholds in the US.

Brian further asserts that the Boston Irish were very different to the New York Irish, in particular, in how they viewed events 3,000 miles away. They were not as sympathetic to the armed struggle. 'Boston was always a hub for west of Ireland people for whom the North was never a huge priority. It may be a generalisation, but by and large, the Irish in Boston weren't as far removed from "home" and were better connected to the sentiments of their brothers and sisters and first cousins than other Irish-Americans who were fourth, fifth, sixth generation.'

Congressman Peter King from New York – a Republican in both the American and Irish sense – was sympathetic to the perspective that was widely shared in his Long Island constituency. A long-serving member of the House of Representatives, King was close to Gerry Adams and Martin McGuinness and once stated that the IRA was 'the legitimate voice of occupied Ireland'. Although the Boston Irish may not have been quite as green on this front, Brian did come under serious pressure in 1981 during the Hunger Strikes. He recalls constituents – Irish-born and others more distant – saying, 'You gotta do something about this, Congressman. This is terrible.'

Brian was a member of the Congressional Friends of Ireland and eventually succeeded Washington representative Tom Foley, a close friend, as its chair when Foley became House Speaker. While that group was certainly nationalist in its orientation, its founder, Speaker Tip O'Neill, and others were hostile to the IRA. Being a member of the Friends group was not without political risk back in Boston because there was also an Ad Hoc Congressional Committee on Irish Affairs, which took a much harder line and was openly sympathetic to the IRA. Some of his backers in Dorchester, Milton and Quincy were much closer in their thinking to the latter and let Brian know it. In his work with the Congressional Friends of Ireland, Brian formed a close personal and working relationship with the highly regarded diplomat James Sharkey, who was then a political counsellor in the Irish Embassy in Washington before being appointed to ambassadorships in Australia, Japan, Denmark, Russia and Switzerland.

Sharkey stresses the significant role played in the 1980s by the Friends group in Congress to further the cause of peace in Ireland. In particular he believes 'their support for in-depth political reform in Northern Ireland and their clear rejection of violence was crucial, given the high-profile alliance between Ronald Reagan and Margaret Thatcher in leading a crusade against communism and international terrorism.' Sharkey recalls that it was 'a very tough time for Irish-Americans on Capitol Hill and the founders of the Congressional Friends of Ireland were wise to enlist a broad, bi-partisan base of young, ambitious politicians who could play a part and respond to constituent pressures stemming from widespread revulsion at the hunger strikes.' Sharkey saw Brian as a prime behind-the-scenes player in the Friends group, particularly when it came to the 'New Ireland Forum', which was the brainchild of John Hume and established by then-Taoiseach Garrett Fitzgerald.

On this front, Sharkey remembers that Speaker O'Neill and Brian helped to arrange for Fitzgerald to give a joint address to the two houses of the US Congress in March of

1984 under the New Ireland Forum banner. And he says that 'the themes were that the forum would be the home for constitutional nationalism and that this was a message of hope from a long-beleaguered Ireland'. Sharkey remembers that 'Fitzgerald's speech was exceptionally well-received' and that, several months later, 'Brian introduced a resolution commending the New Ireland Forum and asking the British government to respond constructively to it. The resolution was passed unanimously by both houses. Brian's initiative and the unanimous support he got for it was an unprecedented and history-making event in Irish-American relations.'

On a lighter, but no less significant, note, Sharkey thinks back to a 1985 visit of the Friends group to Ireland, which was really a celebration of Speaker O'Neill as he prepared to retire. The delegation, which included Brian, Sharkey and several others, got caught in a snowstorm in the Wicklow Mountains and repaired to a pub in the village of Roundwood. There, over pints, the Derry man says that 'the blueprint for what would become the Donnelly Visa was sketched out. Additionally, the idea of establishing an International Fund for Ireland, which has done tremendous good in the North and in border counties, got an airing.' The former ambassador reflects that 'Brian did an awful lot for Ireland, far and above the call of duty'. Because he did, Sharkey jokes that, 'had he run for election here, he might have been president!'

Brian took part in talks and negotiations regularly thereafter in the quest for peace in the North on behalf of the Congressional Friends of Ireland and as a representative of the US government. He was sought out by and grew close to the

1998 Nobel Peace Prize winner and politician, John Hume (and to his wife, Pat), because he was regarded as sensible and because he was close to the congressional leadership. In an early 1990 visit to Dublin, Brian was approached by Mark Durkan, an aide to John Hume who went on to win seats in the Northern Ireland Assembly and in the Westminster Parliament. Durkan informed him about the Birmingham Six. They were Irish men living in the city who had been convicted of bombing pubs and causing the deaths of 21 people and serious injuries to many others. Brian and others met with their families who he says,

> were persuasive in making the case that the convictions were unjust and, because we were in Ireland, I suggested to Bernie Dwyer [a congressman from New Jersey and member of the Friends group] that we jump on a plane to Birmingham and visit these young guys in prison.
>
> It was supposed to be a covert trip. But the British government and then the tabloid press got wind of it. When we got off the plane, there were police and security people everywhere. If looks could kill, Bernie and I would have been dead. They were raging and automatically assumed that we must be Irish-American terrorist supporters. And make no mistake, the IRA was dangerous at that time; the British had a reason to be angry and suspicious. We had to be careful because of the political climate. Reagan and the Republicans were close to Thatcher. The bottom line is that if these guys were guilty, then they deserved what they got and we didn't want our fingerprints near it. But if they weren't, something truly heinous had been perpetrated

against them. And from talking to them in prison and hearing of the lack of evidence, it became clear that the cops' response to the horrible bombings was to go and round up a bunch of Paddys.

When we came out of the prison, the media was lying in wait. They expected that I would speak because I was the Chair of the Congressional Friends of Ireland and, they imagined, a young firebrand Irish nationalist who wouldn't mince my words. Instead, Bernie and I decided that he would make a few comments and that we would get out of there. It worked and we came back to Washington. At the next meeting of our group, there were a number of our members who were wavering and not sure if we should weigh in on this. Bernie swung the room by telling everyone how compelling and believable these six kids were and that they were arrested and convicted simply because they were Irish who couldn't get work at home and had to go to a foreign country that was sometimes hostile to them. And he closed by saying that 'strip away all of our fancy titles and remember what our families' experiences were – not unlike theirs. This is a time to do the right thing.' I filed a resolution robustly condemning the conviction in the House and Joe Biden filed something similar immediately afterward in the Senate. I am proud that we played a part in correcting a horrible miscarriage of justice.

Brian retains the absolute highest regard for the late John Hume.

He was a very impressive guy who I never heard say a bad word about anyone. He was so focused on a positive outcome – no matter how long it took. And the thing is, he lived right in the middle of it; he knew what was going on. I remember arriving to the house in Derry one day with a congressional delegation. The day before, their front door had been blown off. I asked Pat if she wanted to get this fixed quickly. But she said, 'No – I want everyone to see what they did to me and to my children.' They were quite a team. John was an eternal optimist. He really believed – and time has proven him right – that, as technology allowed Northern Ireland to see that most people in the western world don't live in such division or in tangible fear, peace would prevail. He was also a gregarious guy. He really charmed the Boston Irish. And no one could help but cry when he sang 'The Town I Loved So Well'.

The bottom line, according to Brian, is that John Hume was 'single-handedly responsible for the success of the peace process. It never would have gotten over the line if it weren't for John. It was an honour to have met him and to have become his friend.'

Brian also was friendly with the former Tánaiste, Brian Lenihan Sr, who, he says, 'looked like a guy you'd see in a bar on Dorchester Avenue, but was razor sharp and very astute' and with the former Taoiseach, Charles Haughey, who he describes as 'an extremely articulate, capable and respected spokesman for Ireland in the US'. Assessing his dealings with Irish politicians and diplomats in that period, he says:

There may have been controversies associated with some, yet Ireland was incredibly well served by most of them while I was in Congress. They accomplished a tremendous amount. No one should ever forget the difference between Ireland when I first got elected and now. It has changed massively and for the better. They don't need visas to help export their young people safely now. And there was some real political and diplomatic leadership that led to this new reality you're all enjoying now.

It is a source of pride that my uncle played a small part in all of this. Bertie Ahern asserts that Brian's 'contribution to Irish affairs was enormous in difficult times'. Máire Geoghegan-Quinn reflects that, back in the 1980s, 'Irish people knew two American politicians: Ted Kennedy and Brian Donnelly. He has left an extraordinary legacy.' And Niall O'Dowd sums it up for a generation of Irish emigrants: 'Brian Donnelly allowed thousands to live the American Dream and he changed their lives for the better. No politician could do more.'

Anyone acquainted with Brian knows that he would shrug off and downplay these lofty compliments. But I have never heard an Irish person disagree with the sentiments of these three prominent individuals. I have only ever heard their words amplified. I'll leave the last words on Brian Donnelly to Conal Gallagher, originally from Carrickmacross, County Monaghan. He is one of the Donnelly Visa recipients who I hear from periodically.

I ended up in Boston, lived there for a few years, met my wife and now live in Chicago, having raised two boys. I always wanted to send a note of gratitude to your uncle. He provided hope and a new life to many young Irish such as myself when opportunities in the economically depressed Ireland of the 1980s were very poor ... perhaps you'd just mention to him how thankful I am, and what an amazing gift he provided to us. I owe a wonderful life to him.

Since the likes of my uncle, Ted Kennedy, Tip O'Neill, Bruce Morrison and others are no longer championing Irish causes and interests in Washington, DC, there has been much talk of a decline in the influence of Ireland and of Irish-America. This stems to some extent from the fact that there has been no movement at all on the immigration issue since the Morrison Visa programme that followed the Donnelly Visas. Again, immigration is tricky; it is often referred to as the 'third rail' of American politics. The common perception is that something cannot be done specifically for Ireland or for the tens of thousands of undocumented Irish living in the shadows of the US. This is especially the case in light of the massive growth in immigration to the US from Central and South America and their burgeoning political power, as well as an unprecedented national reckoning with race and racism. Moreover, the sense in the US is that Ireland is now a prosperous country that people want to move to, not away from.

Yet there are always young Irish men and women who want to chase the American Dream. Law students come to my office every year for advice as to how they can do so. *Irish Echo* editor Ray O'Hanlon notes: 'Never has the public been more open to reasonable immigration rules and never since the

1920s has the Congress been so bad at delivering it.'[13] Irish-American members of Congress, such as House Ways and Means Committee chair Richard Neal and Brendan Boyle, son of a Donegal emigrant to Philadelphia, have risen to the occasion in the wake of Brexit and the threat it poses to the peace and stability ushered in by the Good Friday Agreement. Through their adroit manoeuvring and forthright advocacy, they elevated the stance of the Congressional Friends of Ireland to the official position of the US House of Representatives and the Senate. One would hope that Irish-American politicians – the 44-year-old Boyle, in particular, who is poised to be the *de facto* leader of Irish-America – will put the same energy into allowing more Irish to come to the US legally. The future of the community and many aspects of the relationship between my two homes depend on it. For one thing, there will be few Americans who will enjoy an upbringing like mine unless the still-closed door opens up a little for the Irish.

13 Ray O'Hanlon, *Unintended Consequences: The Story of Irish Immigration to the U.S. and How America's Door Was Closed to the Irish* (Merrion Press, 2021).

Part Two – Finding My Place

CHAPTER 6

My Early Life

I was born in Boston's Beth Israel Hospital on 18th November 1974, as the city was enveloped in the chaos of the busing crisis. My parents were quite old, for that era, to be welcoming their first child. My father Larry was 40 and my mother Mary (née Flanigan) was just a few weeks shy of reaching the same age. They had met more than a decade previously at a function on Cape Cod, but in my dad's own words, 'I was too dumb to realise I had met the love of my life and settle down.' But she stuck with him through thick and thin and they eventually married in September of 1973.

My mother, who passed away in 2008, was born and raised in the Mossend section of a Scottish town called Bellshill, some ten miles outside of Glasgow. Bellshill was then very much a working-class town and many of the men worked in coal mines. My grandfather, Thomas Flanigan, hailed from a Cavan emigrant family drawn there by the promise of work. He married my grandmother, Christina (née Harvie), and they had four children. Things were not easy for them. World War II was raging; work was hard to come by; and they lost their eldest daughter, Betty, to Hodgkin's disease when she was a teenager. Then, my grandfather passed away very young –

when my mother was just seven, my Uncle Tom was four and my grandmother was pregnant with my Aunt Catherine.

Fortunately, the young widow had family who had left Scotland behind for a new life in the US and had settled in Boston. They scrimped and saved and finally the four of them were able to reunite there as a family in 1954. My mother was 19 when she began her American adventure. Given that their new city was teeming with Irish emigrants, many of those she encountered in her professional and personal ventures, on hearing her twang, automatically assumed that she was from Ireland. Those who were slightly more discerning commonly mistook her Scottish burr for a Belfast accent.

But Mum was an extremely proud Scottish woman who always informed those with any misapprehension about exactly where she was from and took huge umbrage when anyone called her British. Most interestingly, in a dynamic that might sound familiar to Irish people whose family members and friends left the old country behind some time ago, she was an ardent Scottish nationalist. On visits back to Bellshill, I don't think she could fully comprehend the more guarded and cautious views she heard from the people she had grown up with as to the wisdom of Scottish independence from the United Kingdom.

Notwithstanding such differences that distance and time inevitably engender, she stayed close to her roots in Bellshill, and her friends and contemporaries never forgot her. A memory I will forever cherish is being led around Mossend by Mum's oldest friend, Grace Kelly, not long after her death. She had a quick word with an elderly man who then approached me and said: 'Aye, you're Mary Flanigan's wee lad. I can see her in you. I'm so sorry to hear she's gone.'

Mum had a career as a well-regarded legal secretary and worked at a prominent Boston law firm, Lynch, Connolly, Welch & Whitney, for many years until she gave it up not long before I was born. A supportive boss repeatedly encouraged her to attend law school in the evening and to become an attorney. She didn't do so and, while I know she never regretted giving up her career to stay at home with us, I know that a big part of her wished she had taken the offer of a legal education courtesy of her employer that was on the table. Looking back, I really, really would have loved it if she had.

At any rate, with a newborn child, Mum and Dad had to figure out where they were going to settle down. My brother Tommy arrived hot on my heels in March of 1976. We were both baptised in St. Gregory's Church in Dorchester, but the first few years of life were peripatetic. We lived in an apartment above my grandmother and uncle in the Allston neighbourhood of Boston for a couple of years. We also lived in the small town of Hull, across Boston Harbour from the city, in a house my parents had bought right on the water, which we ultimately had to be rescued from when a ferocious storm – known by all New Englanders as the Blizzard of 1978 – hit hard and did serious structural damage to it.

All the while, my Dad was plotting to get us back to his beloved Dorchester, which he had left five years prior when my parents married. He had conversations with a number of acquaintances about returning to St. Gregory's and running for the Boston School Committee as the city was still ravaged by busing. My mother was dead-set against city living in that context, however, and wouldn't budge. As such, in the autumn of 1978, my father relented and they bought the home my brother and his family still live in today in the abutting East Milton. It really was the closest thing possible to being back in Lower Mills; a scenic half-hour walk over Milton Hill would have him at the neighbourhood pub where he had spent a lot of his formative years socialising and where he could still find plenty of familiar faces.

My mother was enamoured by the size of the new home, much bigger than the small council house she had grown up in, and its expansive back yard. Mum also loved East Milton's large and vibrant Roman Catholic parish, St. Agatha, where we went to Mass every week. In those days, observant visitors were prone to joke that one sizable contingent of the invariably thronged congregation would begin the Lord's Prayer in a low volume and a west of Ireland accent, while the rest would project out: 'AAAAH FAATHAH WHO AHHT IN HEAVEN!'

Tommy and I were sent to the parish primary school. That much was preordained. To my mother, a Scottish Catholic who grew up in a working-class area where tensions between Catholics and Protestants ran very high, doing so was a statement of identity and purpose. It didn't matter to her a whit that we were in very different territory. She wouldn't hear of anything else. And so began the extraordinary financial sacrifices my parents made for the two of us in the name of our obtaining the best – and preferably guided by the Catholic faith – education possible.

And they didn't simply leave the education and personal formation, intellectual and spiritual, to St. Agatha School. Every night, Dad read to both me and my brother from a very young age. We soon became voracious readers ourselves and consistently read at a level much higher than was expected for our primary-school grades. Going to Mass every week, not just doing the bare minimum required in order to be deemed eligible to receive the sacraments of First Confession and First Holy Communion, was a central part of our family life. My parents always stressed the importance of setting aside just one hour per week in order to be with God and how being at Mass was a visible affirmation of our gratitude for all that we had and enjoyed. They weren't overly preachy about it, and they would have been the first to admit their own imperfections, but they sought to set an example for us. Both of them leaned on their faith when times were tough. And they wanted us to be able to do the same when we faced challenges in our lives.

The school itself was a strict, yet welcoming, environment in those days. Approximately a third of our teachers were nuns. These nuns and lay teachers did a tremendous job. They were hard on us. They pushed us – figuratively and sometimes literally. And almost to a person, they were very invested in us and in our development. Most of my friends and colleagues on both sides of the Atlantic would have described themselves as 'messers' (in Ireland) or 'show-offs' (in Boston) at some points in their early schooling years. I cannot say the same; to be frank, I was a nerd. By way of example, our house is a five-minute walk from St. Agatha Church and School. The first bell summoning us to class rang out at 8:25 each morning. If we left even a minute after 8:00 a.m., however, I would lose my cool and either break out crying or throw a temper tantrum! Looking back on it, it's mortifying, and I feel awful for my more rational brother and disbelieving mother who had to deal with me.

In one definite sense, this irrational zeal about my schooling paid off. I did well academically. In my final year at St. Agatha, I was named a Scholar of the School by Boston College High School due to my high score on the entrance exam for admission to the Catholic high schools in the Archdiocese of Boston. I was also offered an academic scholarship to Catholic Memorial High School. And this precipitated my having to make the most complicated decision of my 13 years.

Would I accept the scholarship and free my parents from a not insignificant financial burden and make the trek to Catholic Memorial, which was on the other side of the city and where I would know very few students? I was conscious that our regular family trips to Ireland and Scotland had ceased because of impending massive educational expenses. Or would I opt to attend Boston College High School in Dorchester, much closer to home, where many from my class at St. Agatha School were heading? Again, I owe a debt to my parents. They put no pressure on me to accept the scholarship and, looking back on it, were quietly in favour of my choosing BC High. They knew that I was only 13, and a very young 13 at that, and they also recognised that BC High had a superior academic reputation. To this day, it is a cherished institution in the Boston Irish community. After a lot of thought, I informed them that I wanted to go to BC High and apologised for costing them money. I think they were relieved in the end. And it proved to be the right decision for me.

While I worked hard and enjoyed academic success as a boy, what was more important to me and my peers was sporting prowess or lack thereof. My father had been a wonderful athlete; he was the starting quarterback for his high school football team and for a time held city of Boston records in athletics events. My brother took after him and was an excellent natural athlete. Unfortunately, I did not. The amount of hours spent out on our neighbourhood streets and in the local parks – both informally and in organised leagues – playing sports is incalculable. Baseball, basketball, American football and even soccer kept us all occupied.

Many of my friends and contemporaries excelled at one or all of these pastimes. I was small for my age and struggled mightily to keep up. This was incredibly discouraging for me as a young boy. I vividly recall getting quite emotional with my mother on numerous occasions and wishing and praying that I would get better. I certainly worked at it, in particular at basketball. I would regularly arrive at the gym in winter or the outdoor court in summer early in the day and practise shooting until dinner. In so doing, I developed quite a good outside shot and became a competent specialist on this front. The difficulty was getting the shot off as a short and slow prepubescent boy! There were high points in sports in my youth. They were hard-earned and hard to come by. From this vantage point, it seems trifling. But the centrality of sport in terms of the collective measuring of one's self-worth for a boy growing up in the Boston area in the 1980s cannot be underestimated. And for me, it sucked. There is no other way to put it. In another light, by playing sports indefatigably in both recreational and organised settings, I made friends who remain my closest friends today.

The other side of this coin was how big a part of our lives following the Boston sports teams was. The Boston Celtics, at the time, were, together with the Los Angeles Lakers, the dominant force in the National Basketball Association. We idolised Larry Bird and the team's other stars who led them to three championships. The Boston Red Sox broke our hearts in 1986 when, after many, many years of not winning a World Series, they came agonisingly close to breaking the 'curse of Babe Ruth' before falling short. The team had sold Babe Ruth to the rival New York Yankees in 1918 and would not win a World Series until 2004 (something I've gotten accustomed to reminding long-suffering Mayo people in Ireland and America of). The New England Patriots were typically weak, yet made it to one Super Bowl in which they were crushed by the Chicago Bears and William 'Refrigerator' Perry, who captured attention on this side of the Atlantic owing to his outsized frame and persona. And Boston College's football team, led by its diminutive star quarterback, Doug Flutie, gave us all a moment we will never forget when he threw a ball all the way down the field which was caught by Gerard Phelan for a score and a win in what became known as the 'Miracle in Miami'.

Even all these years later and miles away, I still do my best to keep up with how my hometown teams are faring. Texts and phone calls with my childhood pals when we are apart, as well as our gatherings when we get together, invariably revolve around Boston sports. That we have enjoyed fantastic successes in recent years and become the envy or pet hate of so many Americans who begrudge us and our city makes our banter all the sweeter!

CHAPTER 7

Formative Years at Boston College High School

L ooking back, the summer of 1988 may have been the last gasp of an idyllic childhood. To that point, the small world I inhabited revolved largely around St. Agatha Church and School, less than half a mile from my house, and the basketball courts and ball fields that weren't much further away. I was still too young for a part-time job and spent those days clinging to what I had always known before emerging from this happy bubble and beginning my studies at Boston College High School.

BC High, as it is known to everyone in eastern Massachusetts, was founded in 1863 by a Jesuit Priest, Father John McElroy, to educate a growing population of Irish immigrants in the midst of a period of racial and religious hatred in the city. It was initially part of the same institution as the now world-renowned university, Boston College, but later became an independent entity. It was originally situated in the South End neighbourhood prior to relocating to a sprawling harbour-side campus in Dorchester. BC High, for good or for ill, has always been an all-boys school (due disclosure: I believe deeply that it should stay that way) and its graduates include a host of very prominent businessmen, politicians, academics, journalists, doctors, lawyers, writers, professional athletes, entertainers and more. It is regarded as one of the best high schools in Massachusetts and among the best Catholic second-level schools in the US.

Accordingly, while it was an honour to have been accepted there, it was also a daunting prospect. The acceptance letter confirmed that, in order to excel, students at BC High should expect to spend a minimum of three hours every evening on homework. Moreover, I wouldn't be walking down the street to the familiar and cosy confines of St. Agatha anymore; I would be getting on the MBTA (Massachusetts Bay Transit Authority) Red Line subway and travelling a few stops, then undertaking a 15-minute, often numbingly cold and windy walk from the MBTA station, JFK/UMass, to campus. I know that my parents didn't have any doubt about my ability to do the work, yet I was aware that my father, in particular, worried about my level of maturity and capacity to make what was a significant adjustment.

I was just 13, at least a year younger than most of my classmates, a prepubescent boy who stood just a fraction over five feet tall. Even carrying a bag full of books was a challenge. Indeed, years later, my father, with whom I sometimes commuted, told me a story of overhearing a woman on a packed subway car pointing at me after I had managed to weave my way through the crowd and get off. I was making my way down the platform at the JFK Library stop nearest to BC High and she exclaimed to a friend: 'Would you look at him? The bag's bigger than he is!' I was not alone in this regard, but it did make an already tough transition that bit harder.

In that context, while I was angry about it at the time, Dad made a decision on my behalf and without my knowledge that I will forever be indebted to him for. Over the summer, we were asked which foreign language we wanted to study. Naturally, I was curious to ascertain what my friends were doing and would have gone with what the majority selected. Nearly all of them opted for Spanish and I expressed an unthinking preference for it. BC High was always rooted in and prided itself on offering a classical liberal education and my father was determined that I would avail of it. So Latin was the language I 'chose' to study in my freshman year. It's fair to say that the impact on my education was huge.

Among the lasting impressions of the 1988–1989 academic year was sitting in the late Brian Donaher's Latin I class and being asked to conjugate present-tense verbs. Mr Donaher, a superb teacher who was one of many legendary figures at BC High, knew well the psyche of early teen boys and had a keen sense for how to animate them. He would first check the classroom next door to make sure that one of his colleagues, Paul Logan, was teaching there. He would let us know that Mr Logan's class was in progress and then invite us to roar out the verb endings and, in so doing, to disrupt our fellow students. Naturally, we jumped at the opportunity and screamed at the top of our lungs: 'M or O, S, T. MUS, TIS, NT.' Even though Mr Logan mightn't have appreciated it, this was a marvellously ingenious method of getting us to engage with the undeniably boring fundamentals of verb conjugation in Latin. I'll never forget his technique and those present-tense endings will be indelibly etched on my brain until I die. I took to classical languages naturally and wound up studying Latin for all four years at BC High and ancient Greek for the final two.

Mr Donaher was one of many teachers, lay and religious, who made a real difference and inspired me over those four years. Mathematics and science were my weaknesses, so I will always remember the herculean efforts of teachers like Jack Dempsey, Mary Madden and Father Phil Harrigan, S.J. to make chemistry, algebra and geometry more easily understandable for me. Although they couldn't break the graphs, experiments and numbers, which I found incomprehensible but are intrinsically important to those subjects, into words and paragraphs for me, they tried everything else under the sun. Norm Walsh taught me about government and politics and tolerated the fact that I thought I already knew all that there was to learn on that front. I loved English and Dan Shea, Michael McGonagle and Stephen Collins were wonderful, passionate teachers. These men and women could easily have been university professors and some held doctorates. We were incredibly fortunate that their vocation lay in high-school teaching.

There are many others who had a profound effect on me over those four years. Above all, however, BC High instilled an ambition and a work ethic in me. In my first two years there, I was a good student. I was still finding my way and maturing. In between my second (sophomore) and third (junior) years, I resolved to do more. I became far more focused and intense in my studies. In that third year, I achieved a perfect 4.0 grade point average in one term. I have never worked so hard before or since, and it remains the accomplishment in my life I am most proud of. I stayed up late studying most nights of the week and my father regularly had to summon me to bed from my desk in the basement of our house.

I was no angel, however. Like many of my contemporaries, to put it in Boston parlance, my friends and I 'discovered Budweiser' in those teenage years. Much is made of the drinking culture here in Ireland with good reason. But I believe that the culture of drinking excessively in the city's neighbourhoods and the towns and cities to the south of Boston is even stronger – or it definitely was in that era. Some attribute it, fairly or not, to the fact of our Irishness. No matter what it can be put down to, it is undeniable. We dove into it enthusiastically as impressionable adolescents. As a result, my father and mother spent their weeknights telling me to close the books and get to bed and their weekends worrying about what we were getting up to and chastising me after we drank too much and made ourselves sick or got into trouble.

The other non-academic pursuit I stumbled upon while at BC High was what I still think is the best sport in the world, golf. One of my closest friends and I could frequently be found sneaking in a few holes after school. On weekends and on school holidays, we were virtually full-time residents at Presidents Golf Course in Quincy, a tight 18-hole layout with lovely views of the Boston skyline and within walking distance of our family homes. I was foolish enough to begin playing in earnest without the benefit of foundational lessons from a professional, yet somehow managed to get my handicap down to 12 for a time and to shoot regularly in the low 80s, with a number of rounds in the high 70s. Being a junior member at Presidents also disabused me of the notion, widely subscribed to in Ireland to this day, that golf is a wealthy person's pursuit. Presidents had a decidedly blue-collar membership: at the bar, beer came in a can and other drinks were served in plastic cups; and I witnessed more than one on-course disagreement settled in non-gentlemanly fashion, to put it euphemistically. I was able to repay my parents the annual $300 membership fee in small instalments from a part-time job at Burger King. And I couldn't get enough of golf. In truth, I could never have enough of a game that is so much more than just a game.

There was a lot more to my experience at BC High in the late 1980s and early 1990s than chasing academic excellence, the perfect golf swing and a good beer buzz. For one thing, I met different types of people than I grew up around in East Milton. There were guys from the outer suburbs who actually pronounced the letter r; there were black, Hispanic and Asian kids; and there were white kids who stayed behind in the city neighbourhoods that our parents had departed in the wake of the upheaval and chaos engendered by forced busing. A little over a decade on, the city was still reeling from busing and the wounds it inflicted were extremely raw. It was my introduction to the eternally vexed issues of race and racism in America.

Those tensions flared up on several occasions while I was a student at BC High. Rumours that students of colour from the city received preferences over white students from economically disadvantaged backgrounds abounded. The veracity of these widespread anecdotes actually didn't matter anywhere near as much as the perception they created. And this perception led to a culture of resentment that often simmered just below the surface. Every once in a while, what lay beneath boiled over. I remember vividly a clash between groups of African-American students and white students from South Boston. The latter claimed that a first-year student from their tight-knit neighbourhood had been jumped by a number of older black students. There was shouting and screaming of curses and epithets back and forth. The school's teachers and administrators looked on in fear and disgust. Fortunately, the conflict died down that day.

A related sentiment that was as prevalent in Milton and Quincy as in South Boston and Dorchester was that liberal Democrats had abandoned working-class white people and thrown their lot in with African-Americans and other people of colour. Some of that was down to the awful bigotry that forced busing may not have created, yet absolutely fomented. On the other hand, there was a more persuasive element to it. In short, it was reasonably argued that politicians were absolutely correct to stand against discrimination against people of colour and to do everything in their power to eradicate it.

But giving an arbitrary advantage to them – when it came to admission to educational institutions, better access to generous financial aid packages or preferences for highly sought-after jobs in fire and police departments – was seen as tantamount to reverse discrimination against white people, particularly those who were themselves struggling and close to the poverty line. Additionally, these initiatives, no matter how well-intentioned, would only exacerbate bitterness and hostility.

I was, at the time, instinctively sympathetic to this line of argument and often asked my father how the Democratic Party could endorse such a grave betrayal. He was equally mystified. As Senator Edward Kennedy and others vociferously praised these so-called 'affirmative action' policies, I found myself in total disagreement and questioning why my family remained so committed to a party that seemed to now want to give special rights and privileges to some people, just because of their skin colour. My drift to the Republican Party and embrace of a hard-right political ideology that most in Massachusetts found repugnant had begun.

At the same time, my religious faith deepened. I was a student at a distinctly Jesuit high school, where the intellectually rigorous interrogation and subsequent defence of Catholicism were encouraged. My own belief system was far simpler. It was not far from the French philosopher Blaise Pascal's wager: seek to believe in and glorify God; if God does not exist, one loses almost nothing; if God does exist, one gains everything. I attended Mass every week, not because I was forced to, but because I wanted to. It also became an intrinsic part of my identity and, indeed, how I defined myself politically and otherwise. The central aspect of all of this was an outspoken support for the Church's teaching on the sanctity of human life and on the other 'hot button' issues that divided America culturally.

In at least one respect, I subverted my ambition to my faith. Despite having worked so hard and having had a chance to win admission to at least one or two of the Ivy League universities and numerous other highly regarded institutions, I refused to apply to any college or university without a Catholic affiliation. In truth, I was extremely close-minded and viewed the left-wing professoriate, students and general climate I would have encountered on a non-religious campus with undisguised contempt. Had I relented and opted to pursue an undergraduate degree on what would have been very foreign territory, I am not sure I would have lasted, such was the depth of my antipathy toward people who I did not even know. I was nonetheless convinced that they were the enemies of Western civilisation and all that I regarded as sacrosanct.

At any rate, I applied to five Catholic colleges: the College of the Holy Cross, Boston College, Stonehill College (my father's alma mater), Fairfield University and Providence College. The first three are in Massachusetts; Fairfield is in Connecticut and Providence is in Rhode Island. All have very fine reputations. My initial top choice was Boston College. My father, however, was adamantly opposed to my going to BC, mainly because it was just an MBTA journey from home. He wanted me to leave East Milton and gain some independence. He and my mother also thought that, having been made an offer by Holy Cross, a small and prestigious liberal arts college, I would be foolish to turn it down. In my heart, I knew they were right and I decided to accept the offer. It was only 40 miles away from home in the central Massachusetts city of Worcester. But to me at age 17, it seemed like going to the west coast of America.

CHAPTER 8

My College and Law School Years

In the late summer of 1992, I arrived on the beautiful campus of the College of the Holy Cross. Holy Cross – as it's commonly referred to – defines itself as 'a highly selective, liberal arts college renowned for offering a rigorous, personalised education in the Jesuit tradition'. Holy Cross is celebrated in Massachusetts for its blend of strong academics and a proud athletic tradition, as well as for its friendly rivalry with Boston College.

If getting on the MBTA's Red Line to attend BC High had brought me out of my comfort zone in the previous four years, settling in at Holy Cross brought on a massive culture shock. I met people from throughout the north-eastern US and from further afield who were quite different to those that I had grown up around and saw the world through a far broader periscope than I did. It was intimidating.

For one thing, my strong Boston accent was the subject of amusement and ridicule – with some classmates even struggling to understand me. I recall one specific occasion on which I was identifying the location of a student residence hall, Clark, and a friend was convinced I was describing a clock and had no idea what I was talking about! I worked hard to get rid of or at least ratchet down my speech pattern without much success.

My caustic right-wing views also attracted attention for all the wrong reasons. In an American history class focusing on the autobiographies of prominent figures, the professor asked if we had any thoughts or feedback after he had reviewed the outline for the course and the reading materials on our first day. One of the required texts was *The Autobiography of Malcolm X*. I objected and questioned why we were reading something by a man who I deemed a terrorist and an enemy of my country instead of focusing on Martin Luther King and other heroes of the civil rights movement.

Rather than address my issue with Malcolm X, the professor retorted by asking if I was from Dorchester or South Boston. I informed him that my family was from Dorchester and that I had grown up next door in East Milton. It was not the best way to start the semester, for him or for me. We each revealed our biases.

I gravitated toward friends there with similar world views. My roommate for all four years at Holy Cross and I watched the ultra-conservative talk show host Rush Limbaugh on television every night and cheered wildly as he lambasted liberals. I also became friends with several American football players, most of whom were giant men, and with fellow BC High graduates and Boston-area natives finding the adjustment to Holy Cross equally challenging and perplexing compared with what we had known up until that point.

We had a lot of fun together, but it can't be said that we immersed ourselves in the college experience the way our contemporaries did. We scorned the long hairstyles some wore, the 'hippyesque' music and 'college kid' culture they embraced and we venomously opposed the leftist ideology many of our professors frequently espoused. Our mantra was that we chose to attend Holy Cross precisely because we didn't want to hear what we regarded alternatively as anti-Catholic propaganda or grossly unrealistic guff.

And we relished the fact that the residents of Worcester – a mainly working-class community with a complicated relationship to the institution that looked down upon the city from scenic surrounds on top of a hill known as Mount St. James – who we encountered would typically call us normal, unlike most of the students from the college who they came across and almost uniformly despised. We spent the weekends drinking heavily and had more than a few lucky escapes from the law and college authorities.

As ever, I threw myself headlong into my studies from Monday to Friday. The classics department at Holy Cross is one of the highest-rated in the US and best-known in the world. It was a privilege to sit in small classes and be taught by hugely accomplished and brilliant scholars. While I majored in classics – focusing primarily on Latin as a language and on Greek and Roman civilisation – I also took a number of courses in religion, history and political science. I received a magnificent liberal arts education.

In courses on politics and in dialogue in various forums, I was not shy about airing my right-wing views. I enthusiastically backed the re-election of President George HW Bush, despite the fact that my uncle was still a sitting Democratic congressman and a prominent supporter of Bill Clinton. I missed voting in that 1992 election by just a few days, but registered as a member of the GOP on my 18th birthday and even managed to get myself elected to the Milton Republican Town Committee to the chagrin of my family.

As manifested both by my radical political ideology and complete uncertainty about what I wanted for the future, I was young and very immature. On the one hand, I was extremely lucky in that my parents' decades of selfless sacrifice meant that I did not have any student loans. Yet in terms of 'work readiness', a degree in classics is at or near the bottom of the list. I knew that I would need to undertake further study. For a time, I strongly considered pursuing a doctorate in classics and was encouraged to do so by several professors. Any ambition I had in this direction was snuffed out by the denial of tenure – the 'holy grail' in American academia – to two of my favourite professors at the close of my penultimate undergraduate year. At a reception sponsored by grateful students in their honour prior to their departure from Holy Cross, one of them wondered out loud about the future and mentioned, only half in jest, applying to law school.

At that relatively late stage of my undergraduate study, then, I decided that I would take the Law School Admission Test (LSAT) and follow in my father's footsteps. He was vigorously opposed and seriously disappointed when I told him of my plan. Dad was a disenchanted lawyer and didn't think it was the right choice for me either. When I pledged to go ahead regardless, however, he didn't have any better suggestions to offer. Looking back on it, it's strange that neither he nor I nor anyone else I might have listened to put journalism into the mix, given that I was already a full-blown addict (junkie is a more apt term) to politics, news and current affairs. Coming from a political family who generally disdained journalists – in his own inimitable style, Uncle Frank was fond of saying that 'a cup of coffee and a slice of pie will buy you a newspaper guy' – the prospect of my having a career in the fourth estate never got remotely close to Dad's radar screen.

At any rate, I applied to three law schools: Boston College Law School, Boston University School of Law and Suffolk University Law School. I also studied belatedly for the LSAT, without the benefit of a preparatory course that most serious applicants take. I did reasonably well under the circumstances and, based on my very strong marks at Holy Cross, hoped to be admitted to all three law schools. Regrettably, one of my referees neglected to submit a letter in support of my application materials in a timely fashion and, because my application was deemed to have been received after the deadline as a result, I was placed on the waiting list by BC Law and BU Law.

I was lucky to be accepted at Suffolk Law. My father advised that I should defer the year and hence gain entry to either or both of the higher-ranked schools in all likelihood, but I was desperate to continue with my education without delay and was appreciative that Suffolk offered me a place in the class of 1999. In late summer of 1996, just a few months after graduating from Holy Cross, I began pursuit of a Juris Doctor degree at the law school on Boston's Beacon Hill, then situated directly behind the Massachusetts State House. My great-uncle Frank Kelly had learned his trade at Suffolk Law, along with countless other politicians and judges in the state.

And once he accepted that I wasn't for turning, my father advised me to conceive of the three years ahead as being akin to a trade school. He warned that it would be a very different teaching and learning experience from what he described wryly as 'luxuriating in two dead languages' at Holy Cross. The very first day at Suffolk Law brought that reality home for me in an unenviable way. In a first-year property law class of approximately 120 students – I found myself in a daunting setting surrounded by ambitious people, all of whom held undergraduate degrees with many also holding postgraduate degrees in other disciplines or having the benefit of years of professional experience – the professor opened proceedings as follows: 'Is there a Lawrence Donnelly here?'

I raised my hand, foolishly thinking that the professor knew my father or was simply making an introduction. Instead, he asked me to outline the facts of a case and the resulting precedent with respect to a bailment, a feature of the common law of personal property in the US. It was the most trying baptism by fire of my life. This professor was a traditionalist and I was the first student to get a full dose of the law school Socratic Method, in which first-year students are cold-called and interrogated about the facts and decisions of court cases.

Thankfully, I had done the assigned reading carefully. I managed to battle through the nerves and comported myself reasonably well for 50 minutes that seemed like an eternity. I struggled initially with the nuances of law study and legal writing – something I never fail to mention when teaching legal skills to my own students – yet improved as the first year went on. I did well, managed to get a summer job at a law firm, Curtin, Murphy & O'Reilly, where a classmate of my father's was a founding partner, and earned a coveted spot on the staff of the *Suffolk Transnational Law Review*. I had planned to apply to transfer to BC or BU after my first year, but after working so hard, in particular in a gruelling competition to gain a position on the law review, I decided to remain at Suffolk.

I loved studying law there. After figuring out the lie of the land and developing my own approach to it, my performance and all-important class ranking improved further. Suffolk Law's emphasis is on the 'real world' practice of law and experiential learning. This was invaluable for me and helped shape my career trajectory. And the countless hours labouring individually and collaboratively with capable, diligent colleagues to produce two editions of an outward-looking law review annually – first researching and writing two published articles and then serving as an editor and mentor in my final year – satiated my appetite for legal theory and engendered a passion for comparative law. I was invited for numerous interviews with some of the city's leading law firms for lucrative summer associate positions that typically lead to an offer of employment after graduation.

I evidently failed to impress in meetings with partners at these so-called 'white shoe' firms, though, because I was never invited back for a second interview. Nerves probably got the better of me. In truth, knowing that these very highly paid jobs entailed working a ridiculous amount of hours and having no life at all and that, owing to the pervasive snobbery within these firms, a Suffolk Law graduate with an Irish surname and a Boston accent would always be looked at somewhat askance, I wasn't overly disappointed.

At the same time, my involvement in politics and government deepened significantly. I was elected to Milton's representative town meeting at the close of my first year in 1997. Months later I was appointed to the town's warrant or finance committee. The latter was an enormous commitment in that the committee has responsibility for making recommendations on budgets for all departments and meets for at least two hours twice a week for most of the year. I also worked on my Uncle Brian's unsuccessful campaign for the Democratic nomination for Governor of Massachusetts in 1998 and then managed the (again unsuccessful) campaign of a friend for local office in 1999. All the while, I was a full-time law student and worked as many hours as possible at Curtin, Murphy & O'Reilly.

It was an incredibly busy three years with all that I had going on. That left little time for socialising. There was no sign of a girlfriend, not even close. My mother's constant prayers that someone nice would come along went unanswered. It was also difficult in that most of my friends from my childhood in East Milton and from Holy Cross were enjoying the spoils of their first professional jobs with no responsibilities. I had very little money and was taking on debt to fund my education. Even if I had to stay at home a lot or shamelessly 'borrow' money from my friends that they knew they would never get back, they were three great years. It should be said that Boston was still quite an affordable place back then for a young graduate student. Unlike today, there were bargains aplenty for eating and drinking out because the city still had lots of working-class, long-time residents and businesses had to cater to their limited budgets.

Studying law academically and working in the field, as well as being so heavily engaged in politics and government, also made me re-evaluate my arch-conservative belief system. In short, it made me realise that not everyone had the relatively carefree existence with a stable family life and financial and other support that I had always taken for granted. Emerging from Holy Cross, I may have been 21 years old and technically an adult, yet I was a spoiled, overly opinionated know-it-all when it comes down to it. What I was exposed to during those three years engendered a fairly rapid maturation process. In short, I started to cop on to some of the uncomfortable realities of life.

Not everyone had parents who had enough to pay for them to attend private schools throughout their childhood and get them through four years of higher education with no debt. Not everyone saw their parents strive every day to set a good example for them in how they lived their lives. Not everyone resided in a community where violence and discord were rare. And not everyone grew up with the myriad advantages conferred on me just by virtue of having white skin. My thinking on all of these fronts, in particular on the issues of race and racism, changed drastically while I was at Suffolk Law. I was still a committed Catholic, still socially conservative, but I was slowly coming to reject many of the tenets I had for so long held deeply about just about everything else. Slowly but surely, my family's Democratic Party was calling me back.

CHAPTER 9

Returning to the Democratic Party

My being a registered Republican was always awkward and a major impediment to any chance I had for running for any office beyond representative town meeting member. Notwithstanding the badgering of family, friends and acquaintances, I persevered and robustly defended my steadfastly hard-right beliefs on both economic and cultural matters. Most of these exchanges ended with my counterparts shaking their heads. My father, ever the pragmatist, couldn't figure out why I would deliberately take myself out of the game if and when vacancies in elected positions arose locally.

It was, I suppose, because I subscribed so fanatically to conservative philosophy. That bible of the American right, *National Review* magazine, arrived at the house every two weeks and I promptly devoured it. It shaped my thinking and fuelled my regular, unprompted, unwanted outbursts against the dominant leftist thinking in Massachusetts. Many of my male contemporaries gravitated similarly to conservatism. In hindsight, there was an odd mix of machismo and intellectual snobbery to it. I also grew apart from the GOP Town Committee of which I was a member as it became dominated by moderates who combined fiscal prudence with social liberalism, which I found anathema.

But even before I was a law student, doubts had begun to creep into my mind. Some of the questioning stemmed from the part-time job I held at a Burger King near my house during high school and college. With a father who was a judge and an uncle who was a prominent politician, more glamorous and less taxing employment, as well as a host of attractive internships, lay within the relatively easy reach of a phone call. But Dad was resolutely opposed to that and thought it extremely important that I gain experience at the bottom – working hard in a job that was quite embarrassing for a teenager and making the minimum wage. Not for the first time, he was right.

My fellow employees were a diverse range of people. Young people like me studying and earning a little money. Bored older people retired from their first career and unable to cope without working. Full-time workers, many of whom were people of colour and/or immigrants who didn't speak English well, doing their best to make a better life for themselves and their families under trying circumstances. I learned a lot more than how to dress a burger or take orders at the drive-thru. It made me understand that some people struggle just to get by each and every day, and will do so for their entire lives.

The men and women I laboured alongside would never earn big salaries, drive nice cars or be more than one pay cheque away from homelessness. All they could do was scrape by and hope their hard work would lead to a better life for their children. Seeing their tough situations and witnessing their fundamental decency, kindness and optimism notwithstanding their unenviable lot in life didn't sit nicely alongside my overarching laissez-faire economic outlook or oft-repeated mantra that those who called for the wealthy to pay more in taxes than the poor were socialists. These working poor people didn't want a hand-out; they wanted and deserved a hand up. Again looking back, there was actually very little that differentiated them from the Irish immigrants to the US who preceded them.

Another factor, which may seem totally off the wall at first, was my gravitation to the message offered by Pat Buchanan in his insurgent Republican primary campaign against President George HW Bush in 1992 and his second bid for the White House in 1996. How could sympathy for the sentiments of a commentator-turned-presidential-wannabe, who is uniformly labelled as far-right, lead one to the Democratic Party? In short, I found his outlook on economics and foreign policy far more compelling than conservative orthodoxy.

On economics, Buchanan assailed the embrace of both parties – at the behest of wealthy donors and special interests – of so-called free trade deals like the North American Free Trade Agreement (NAFTA), which he correctly predicted would displace millions of well-paid men and women in the manufacturing sector and eviscerate communities across the country as a result. On foreign policy, he argued trenchantly against the use of military force unless as a last resort and disputed the notion that America should be the world's policeman. I couldn't have agreed more and increasingly came to despair at the disproportionate influence of moneyed interests and the revolting military-industrial complex. And this was especially evident in the Republican Party establishment that Buchanan so annoyed in his longshot campaigns. He actually stole the Democrats' clothes on this front.

Then, at Suffolk Law, which has long prided itself on providing access to the legal profession for non-traditional students, I met a broad cross-section of women and men pursuing their dreams of entering the legal profession. It was fascinating to speak with classmates and to hear their life stories and reasons for going to law school. As well as recent graduates with lawyers in their families like mine, there were people who were the first in their families to obtain an undergraduate degree, single parents juggling several balls simultaneously and people who had had a bad experience of the law and legal system and were motivated by a desire to either right manifest wrongs or avenge what they personally perceived to have been travesties. It was a different student body altogether to what I had found at Holy Cross.

Moreover, one thing that should emanate naturally from legal education is a sense of awe that comes with putting oneself forward to be a lawyer, an officer of the court with a special standing in society. A second is a cognisance that, while lawyers are charged with safeguarding the institutions and instruments sacred to the administration of justice, they are not perfect and other lawyers have a vital responsibility to hold the system to account when they fail. Both permeated the air at Suffolk Law and surfaced repeatedly in the lecture theatre in subjects like criminal and constitutional law. Additionally, the law school's focus on skills training and on clinical legal education – in which students learn by doing and, by working on behalf of indigent clients, facilitate access to justice and the advancement of the public interest – hammered home the reality that, in the US, the deck is often stacked against those on the margins of society.

It may have been a step down from these lofty ideals, yet a course I took in Law and Public Policy that was taught by the then-Speaker of the Massachusetts House of Representatives, Thomas Finneran, had an impact in a different way. The Speaker, who inherited my uncle's seat in the state legislature when Brian moved on to Congress, was a conservative Democrat who was scorned equally by Republicans and the more progressive elements in his own party. His common-sense approach to the issues we dealt with, which typically involved highlighting the obvious drawbacks in the analysis of those on the poles and the wisdom of occupying the centre ground in most instances, was very persuasive. It helped to affirm that there was space for me in the Democratic Party and that it was important to preserve that centrist space within the party.

This teaching and learning environment was complemented well by my 'real world' legal work at Curtin, Murphy & O'Reilly. The firm engages primarily in the defence of self-insured entities in litigation resulting from workplace injuries, injuries suffered on business premises and claims of discrimination, but also represents plaintiffs in similar court actions. In assisting the firm's attorneys on the cases they worked on, primarily through legal research, drafting memoranda of law, and contributing to court submissions, the hardscrabble existences of plaintiffs, as well as the low-paid employees of the entities the firm represented, were frequently manifest.

And, of course, my own engagement in politics helped to change my perspective. Serving as an elected Town Meeting Representative and on the Milton Warrant Committee made me get to grips with the facts that local government typically runs on a shoestring. Despite the widespread perception in the US that those who work in the public sector are overpaid, 'fat cat' bureaucrats, most I came across were on low salaries, yet worked very hard. The vast majority did so out of a love for and commitment to their community. In listening annually to their heartfelt pleas for further funding, it was always extraordinary to hear, on the one hand, all that they managed to do on scant resources, and depressing, on the other, to have to refuse the justified requests of eminently deserving local government departments in many instances.

I was fortunate to get this ground-level exposure and insight. It transformed my thinking. For I, like most Americans, would have demanded and expected high-quality public services. Unlike people in Western Europe or elsewhere, however, we Americans are practically programmed to object to paying for them and far too willing to buy into the narrative promoted by the right that government is invariably bloated, inefficient and not worthy of investment which will inevitably be wasted. This broadly unsubstantiated notion does a real disservice to those within government who work so hard and, ultimately, to the communities that their inhabitants profess to care so much about.

At a personal level, it also struck me that the anti-government strain of American conservatism was directly at odds with what I had seen five days a week when I lived at my parents' house. My father was a government lawyer for many years before garnering appointments to administrative judgeships at the state and federal levels. He was a very able and well-respected lawyer who surely could have made a lot more money in the private sector. Even allowing for my bias, there are scores of talented individuals who work for the government and who, if they were to depart, would be a real loss to the people they serve. Anti-government slogans and scapegoating public sector employees might be effective politically, but doing so is generally inaccurate.

Finally, there was my work on political campaigns for Democrats. In mid-1997, having left his post as US Ambassador to Trinidad and Tobago, there was considerable speculation that my Uncle Brian would seek his party's gubernatorial nomination in 1998. I may still have been a registered Republican, but I was going to do whatever I could to support his bid, no matter what. And the first step in that regard was switching my party affiliation. That was difficult in many respects because of the unease I still had with the Democratic Party and initially I cast myself as a 'Jimmy Kelly Democrat'.

Kelly was an extremely conservative Boston City Councillor from South Boston who came to prominence as one of the leaders in the anti-busing movement and never backed down from a fight with people he regarded as 'pointy-headed liberals and social engineers'. Many of his fellow Democrats were appalled by him – though he was an unwavering champion of his working-class constituents, not just in South Boston, but also in Chinatown, which was a part of his council district and where he was beloved by the neighbourhood's long-time residents.

At any rate, I did the basics in my uncle's campaign: making phone calls, attending functions and debates, holding signs. On the day he formally announced in a Boston hotel ballroom, the huge sign hanging on the wall behind the stage he addressed the crowd from – 'Brian Donnelly: Democrat for Governor' – regrettably came undone and fell to the floor. Sadly, it was something of metaphor for what was my uncle's last hurrah. Brian had been gone too long and we couldn't raise enough money, but we battled on regardless and finished a distant third in the end. Being the precocious 23-year-old I was, I thought that I would have been better on strategy than the veterans in charge, but this was a straight uphill quest in a state that had changed so much so quickly in the years since Brian had been an officeholder. Still, though, it was an extremely valuable learning experience.

The next year, I was asked by a candidate for the Milton Select Board to run his campaign. The members of the select board are the chief elected officials and executive officers of the town. The candidate, the late Edward Duffy, was from East Milton, where he was a well-known neighbourhood activist, and a long-time town employee, as well as a representative town meeting member. Eddie was a great guy with a lot of friends in town, a Boston College alumnus and lifelong resident of East Milton. He was passionate about our neighbourhood, which was then far less salubrious than other areas of the town. Our utility poles and power lines were above ground; our properties were smaller; and our identity was quite different. Our Irishness, for one thing, was more visible and tangible in the streets, in the parks and in the main shopping district, East Milton Square. We would never say we were from Milton – we were from East Milton, and that was saying something in itself. Despite the fact that East Milton was home to a substantial share of the population, many of my neighbours long felt unrepresented and even looked down upon at Town Hall.

Running in a relatively crowded field as the only person from the neighbourhood, these themes were deployed subtly and not so subtly throughout. Eddie was a very bright guy, but arguably not as polished or articulate as some of his opponents. My strong idea was that he shouldn't hide from this, but deliberately play it up because it would resonate with voters who would find him easier to relate to – especially the Irish immigrants, refugees of Boston's busing crisis and 'townies' who were still a big part of the town's electorate at this stage. My hope was that the others would divvy up more affluent and left-leaning support and we would have a lane pretty much to ourselves. What I didn't anticipate or see coming – in hindsight I should have – was that one candidate whose family had been active in local politics for some time would emerge and take the overwhelming share of those votes. There wasn't much of a spread.

In the end, while Eddie won East Milton by positively monstrous margins, it still wasn't enough to get him over the line. It was quite disappointing for him, having put his heart and soul into it, and for me as a young man trying to make a name for himself, but that's politics. Afterward, we had a few beers and tried to make the best of a bad result.

I had to move beyond that loss in April of 1999 quickly. I had my final-year law school exams to cram desperately for. Thankfully, they went well. I graduated from Suffolk Law in May and then faced into two months of intense preparation for the Massachusetts bar exam. As most American lawyers would tell you, the experience of studying for and then sitting the bar exam is one best put out of one's head as soon as it is over. For June and July, the crucial preparatory course and concomitant individual study and practice test-taking were akin to working a demanding, full-time job in the scorching heat with a very dark and ominous cloud lurking overhead.

Virtually every already qualified lawyer I spoke to that summer assured me that I would pass; their easy confidence didn't erase the lingering doubts that consumed me at night. And strolling nervously into a massive conference room in Boston's World Trade Centre with thousands of other exam takers for two days in late July was something I'll never forget. I overcame a shaky, sweaty hand and got through it without incident. I had a blowout week on Cape Cod with the crew from East Milton immediately thereafter. And – fortunate to have been offered a position as an associate at Curtin, Murphy & O'Reilly, where I had worked for the previous two years – I walked into my very own office on the 10th floor of a striking building in downtown Boston as an all but qualified lawyer in August of 1999. Those were heady days.

CHAPTER 10

My Practice as a Lawyer and Relocation to Ireland

At Curtin, Murphy & O'Reilly, I worked alongside excellent lawyers and professional support staff. Two mentors at the firm who truly made a lasting impression were one of the founding partners, Bill Murphy, and its managing partner, Paul Moretti. I draw on things they taught me by example to this day. In short, I learned from Bill and Paul that it is obviously important to strive to be a good lawyer, yet it is also important to be a fundamentally decent and fair person at the same time. I don't think anyone in Boston's legal community who has encountered the two men could question either their capacity as advocates or the quality of their character.

Curtin, Murphy & O'Reilly is a small to mid-sized firm by Boston standards – between 12 and 15 lawyers – and is engaged exclusively in civil litigation. In particular, the firm specialises in the defence of self-insured businesses and educational institutions against claims filed in state and federal courts and administrative bodies for workplace injuries, injuries incurred by customers on their premises and for discrimination in employment. The firm also represents plaintiffs in these areas.

As a law student, I spent most of my time undertaking legal research in connection with motions and appellate briefs that I increasingly played a role in drafting. Unlike law practice in Ireland, a significant portion of legal argument in American litigation is conducted 'on the papers'. Carefully and persuasively drafted written submissions – bolstered by comprehensive research of germane precedent – are an absolute necessity and often tell the tale. These submissions underpin what is commonly called motion practice. Motions to dismiss at the start of a case or for summary judgment later on, after the plaintiff and defendant have exchanged relevant information about the facts and background to the lawsuit, are common in the US. Decisions on such motions tend to shape the future contours of the dispute, which could include settlement, a joint agreement to pursue an alternative means of resolution or proceeding to a full trial on the merits.

I greatly enjoyed conducting legal research, especially the 'needle in the haystack' type where I had to uncover an obscure precedent to assist in a client's case, and writing memoranda of law which were incorporated into motions and appellate briefs. This satiated my academic interest in and passion for the law. I found that the exchange of information between the parties to a case, known as discovery, decidedly did not. Typically, on commencement of a lawsuit in this area of practice, requests would be filed by both sides seeking a huge amount of information relating to the alleged facts and key individuals and entities. Upon receipt of the request, discovery began. It was necessary to marshal together all of the crucial facts and documents, then determine what should be lawfully given over and what should be withheld and/or deemed privileged.

As opposed to the other aspects of law practice that I found stimulating, my limited exposure to the discovery process as a student was excruciating. The tasks of trawling through boxes of documents, speaking to disinterested employees (if on the defence's side) or less-than-truthful clients (if on the plaintiff's side), examining internal company policies and procedures and ascertaining if sought-after materials needed to be produced or not pursuant to the rules were uniformly dreadful, exhausting and mind-numbing. Naturally, every job has its positives and negatives. But my aversion to the process of discovery of documents and related spats between parties to litigation – even as a law student – was so strong that I knew I could not ever be happy if it consumed even a smallish percentage of my working life. Put simply, it was not what I went to law school for.

As late August of 1999 turned into September, it felt extremely odd, at age 24, to not be going 'back to school' for the first time ever. It was nice to finally be earning a decent, full-time wage and to be able to enjoy myself with my friends on weekends without constantly worrying about money. And we certainly did.

Our weekend routine involved hitting the old-school Irish bars that then lined Dorchester Avenue on Friday night, heading downtown on Saturday afternoon and staying out until the wee hours and then spending Sunday in various pubs listening to Irish music and watching sports, kidding ourselves that we would be fine when the alarm clock went off first thing on Monday morning. As an aside, 'old Boston' was still very much alive and kicking. It wasn't ridiculously expensive; it was full of Irish emigrants; and it certainly wasn't posh or fancy. In short, we may have been the last generation to get to enjoy the city – both its downtown and its neighbourhoods – that our parents knew and loved so well. From another vantage point, there was no diversity (I could probably count on two hands the number of African Americans I encountered on those wild weekends) and the racial animosity stemming from busing lingered, sadly yet sometimes palpably, in the air.

This was all great fun, but looking back, I still wonder how we did it. That November, I got the excellent news that I had passed the bar exam. I was sworn in as an attorney in Boston's historic Faneuil Hall with my parents looking on with pride. And naturally, immediately after I had sworn the oath and signed my name in the register, the gang from East Milton decided the occasion was ample cause for another night of celebration in the numerous nearby bars we held court in.

One of the topics of conversation that night was the wedding of a first cousin of one of my closest friends that we had all been kindly invited to the following April. My friend's cousin was from Galway and had been living in East Milton for several years, but was returning home to get married to a fellow Galwegian before coming back to their lives in America. With some money of my own for a change and not having been to Ireland in a number of years because of the financial constraints imposed by higher education, I was a definite from the get go. In the end, from our crew, it was only me and the cousin of the groom who boarded an Aer Lingus flight in the spring of 2000.

I didn't know it at the time, but attending that wedding changed the course of my life. We had the time of our lives. Between the multiple-day party that was the wedding, the novelty of being somewhere different and the warm welcome and hospitality we were the beneficiaries of throughout, that vacation in Galway was extraordinary in every conceivable way. It was the first time I had ever left Boston for any length of time that I did not want to come back to it. On returning home, we vowed to go back as soon as we could and even discussed the possibility of moving there for a time. Both of us had Irish passports and were single, so why not?

The seed had been planted. Our friends scoffed at the notion whenever we put it out there. Although I can't speak definitively for my travelling companion, I was deadly serious. Meanwhile, my career in law practice trundled along. Owing at least partly to an unexpected departure of one of the lawyers from the firm, the role I had expected to play at Curtin, Murphy & O'Reilly was not as I had envisaged. I was given an admittedly small number of cases to take charge of, a significant responsibility for a newly minted lawyer, and did the best I could with them. I continued to enjoy researching and writing court submissions and particularly enjoyed arguing points of law in motion hearings in court. I also came to like one part of the discovery process: taking the oral depositions of parties and witnesses in litigation in the presence of counsel for the other side and a stenographer who recorded proceedings.

I had some early successes in practice. I drafted a memorandum in response to a motion by one of Boston's top employment lawyers, argued it in court and prevailed. I contributed to a number of winning appellate briefs. A judicial colleague of my father commented to him about how well-written and compelling a submission of mine was. There were lighter, memorable moments, too. A judge, seeing a nervous wreck of a rookie lawyer standing before her, addressing a shaving cut that refused to stop bleeding with a jagged piece of toilet paper, opened proceedings by expressing her wish – to the laughter of the court personnel and other lawyers present – that 'Mr Donnelly's argument will be at least as incisive as his razor obviously was.' On another occasion, I had to use all of my powers of persuasion to prevent an extremely volatile and large client from erupting at a deposition where I was on my own and the other parties had six, vastly more experienced lawyers peppering him with questions.

But I did not like the job and, to my shame, didn't always give it my all. It was making me miserable. I hated looking at case files. At my first actual trial, I did horribly and lost the case. I loathed the tedium of the discovery process, the haggling that often went on in settlement negotiations and the stress that flowed from my full knowledge that a mistake could have dire consequences for a client, for the firm and for me. I desperately did not want to disappoint the great people who I worked with and who had given me responsibility and opportunity that my law school classmates working at larger firms and elsewhere had not been granted. It wasn't long before I knew that I wasn't going to last in law practice – at least not in litigation – and that an exit strategy would have to be devised swiftly. I didn't feel like a failure; I fully recognised that this wasn't where I wanted to be, however.

My father's warnings that attending law school wasn't a good idea reverberated in my head.

The big difficulty was that I did have more than $50,000 worth of law school debt and would have to find gainful employment – either in a different sort of legal career or in another field altogether. For a time, I even pondered if I had a religious vocation. Was this professional frustration that bordered on humiliation on the inside after many years of studying so hard God's way of telling me that my real calling was the priesthood? At any rate, while doing enough to keep my head above water as a lawyer, I thoroughly investigated what opportunities there might be in Ireland. I reached out to every contact suggested to me and planned a second trip in March of 2001 to see what I might be lucky enough to hit upon. Once again, it was wonderful. But it was an abject failure in terms of charting a new course for my career.

I was disheartened. Yet on coming back to the office, I decided to work as hard as I could and adopt a new attitude to law practice. Shortly thereafter, I received a letter of rejection in response to an application for a teaching post in the Faculty of Law (as it then was) at the National University of Ireland, Galway. I was not at all surprised. The formal letter, though, was followed by an email from Professor Gerard Quinn which mentioned a fellowship the faculty awarded annually to an American lawyer to teach legal skills modules to first- and second-year students. In the past, the fellowship had always been awarded to Harvard Law School graduates. Professor Quinn was a Harvard Law graduate himself and, in his time living in the Boston area, became well aware of Suffolk Law's sterling reputation in legal skills teaching. In light of my blend of strong academic credentials, practical experience and affinity to the west of Ireland, he thought that I would be a good fit and urged me to consider applying. I did not have to think twice about it, applied immediately and was offered the one-year fellowship.

My parents, who had borne the brunt of my 'early career crisis' and knew well how badly I needed to take my life in a radically different direction, were over the moon, even if they were sad that I would soon be separated from them by an ocean. My father, naturally, couldn't resist making a wisecrack. 'Your grandmother would be sending the men in white coats for you.' And based on tales passed down by her children, I have no doubt that she would have been revolted by her grandson's decision. Indeed, she was reared on stories about the ghastly place her family had escaped and thus had no interest in Ireland. She went once, began the vacation to her home place by ridiculing the people 'driving on the wrong side of the road' and re-booked her flight to return to Boston early. Her sentiments were not uncommon for Irish-Americans of her generation who desperately wanted to be fully immersed in the new country and forget about the old. That said, the Galway of 2001 was a very different place than the one she and others ever envisaged.

After a few days of prevaricating, I broke the news to Bill and Paul at the firm and, in so doing, let them know that I was leaving not only because I had this unique offer from NUI Galway, but also because I had recognised that law practice was not for me. At the same time, though, I let them know how grateful I was for the break they had given me and how much I had learned from them in a short period. I pledged to continue to progress my cases in the summer of 2001 and to write transfer memoranda for the lawyers who would be assigned to take them on. I also prepared to relocate and take on a very different type of job.

Then, as luck would have it, I met someone in late July, just six weeks or so before I would be boarding an Aer Lingus flight. It was on a booze cruise around Boston Harbour sponsored by one of the Irish pubs we frequented. Karen was a very attractive, bright, Italian American teacher from north of the city. Anyone at all familiar with eastern Massachusetts will know the vast cultural differences between the north and south shores and those of Italian and those of Irish heritage. We had a long conversation about many things, including politics, that night and exchanged contact details. While most young women would have run a mile from a young man outlining his reasons for vigorously opposing embryonic stem cell research, she was actually interested. I was different to most of the guys she had dated, to put it mildly.

We were both in a strange place; I was moving to Ireland and she was moving to Washington, DC to begin a PhD in education at American University. Even though we knew a day of reckoning and separation was fast approaching, we didn't hold back and fell in love very quickly. For someone who had never been in a serious relationship before, it was a wonderful summer romance and it flew by in what seemed like an instant. This was a new wrinkle that I had no reason to expect and there is no denying that it complicated things significantly.

Both Karen and I were quite emotional in the waning days of August as we talked about what might lie ahead of us and if it was worth endeavouring to maintain the strong connection we had rapidly established. We resolved that we would try a long-distance relationship.

It was always going to be tough to leave my family and friends behind. Leaving behind my first serious girlfriend made it even harder. It was, therefore, with a wide range of heartfelt emotions that I nursed a beer at Logan Airport's Terminal E while waiting to board a plane for Shannon in early September 2001.

Life in Galway and Work at NUIG

I was greeted that early morning at Shannon Airport by my cousin Siobhán and her husband, John, who my parents had told about my impending relocation to Galway. Siobhán had spent a considerable amount of time in Boston during and after university and, even though she hadn't seen me for a decade, recognised me immediately. And I knew her, too, from the many evenings she spent with us in East Milton and from our visits to her family home in north Galway. Needless to say, it was great to see a familiar face and to have a lift waiting on arrival.

The Murphy family are distant relations of ours – Siobhán's late father, John, was a first cousin of my grandmother – but that day commenced a renewal of that relationship and they have been wonderful to me ever since. In particular, weekend visits to Siobhán's home in Boyle, Co. Roscommon, to her brother John in Sligo and to my cousin Paddy, who lives with his family next door to his mother, Kathleen, in Lavally (halfway between Tuam and Dunmore in north Galway) on the farm that is my 'home place' in Ireland, have become a treasured feature of my life. My family was good to them when they came to Boston; they have repaid the kindness tenfold at this stage.

That September morning, we drove straight to the beautiful campus of the National University of Ireland, Galway. It was awe-inspiring to pass the quadrangle and its magnificent courtyard surrounded by ivy-covered walls, something that wouldn't be out of place in Oxford or Cambridge. We were guided by John, a solicitor and graduate of the law school, who knew exactly where to go and we got the details of the bed and breakfast where I would be staying for the next several days prior to finding my own accommodation. I thanked John and Siobhán so much for their assistance and went to bed for a few hours. I next strolled into a city I had become somewhat familiar with on my trips to get some dinner. But it felt different. Galway was now home.

The first of many rude awakenings came the following morning. Eager to throw myself into my teaching, I woke up at 6 a.m., showered and put on the suit that had been my uniform for the past two years in Boston and sought to get into the office for seven. Unfortunately for me on a rainy morning, however, the door was locked and the lights were still dim. Thankfully, a member of the cleaning staff let me in. I learned an important lesson on the very first day: life starts a little bit later in the west of Ireland than it does in the north-eastern United States.

At any rate, I spent hours painstakingly readying my first lectures in a very different environment and met a number of very welcoming, friendly and impressive colleagues. The first day of the semester was Monday, the 10th of September and I had a lecture in the morning and one in the evening. I was beyond nervous to assume this new role. I made a couple of embarrassing mistakes and butchered the pronunciation of the Irish names that would take me a while to get my head around. Unlike American law students, these were undergraduates who were far more reticent to speak in class, probably due to their age and, equally probably, due to a cultural difference I would have to get used to: Irish law students aren't as outspoken, loud or confident as those I had soldiered with at Suffolk Law.

The nerves, uncertainty and bungling that were visible for all to see notwithstanding, I still managed to get through it without major incident. Like everyone else on the planet, I had not the remotest notion of what would transpire in the following 24 hours.

On September 11th, 2001, I went to the office and spent much of the morning reflecting on what had been effective and what had not during the first lectures I had ever given on the previous day. Shortly after lunch, a colleague alerted me that a plane had crashed into the World Trade Center in Manhattan. I was taken aback, but did not think much of it initially. Surely, this was a small plane that had lost control and met an unfortunate end. When I saw the footage, however, it immediately became clear that something far more dastardly was underway. I retreated to the bed and breakfast to watch the terrifying coverage for the rest of the day. I attempted to contact my parents, brother and friends who I thought would have information about the people we knew who were based in New York. I didn't have much luck. I also tried to reach

Karen who I feared could be in danger in Washington. In truth, the rumours that were flying around and the related panic that ensued were so widespread that it was impossible to know who was safe and who was not. I wished that I was home.

Eventually, I reached everyone and was hugely relieved that they were all OK. But it was clear that things had changed. On a long weekend trip to Washington, DC to see Karen a month later, the sight of military personnel patrolling Dulles International Airport with high-powered weaponry was shocking and intimidating. I returned home for Christmas as well and had another stark reminder of the ramped-up security when I went into downtown Boston for Curtin, Murphy & O'Reilly's annual Christmas party.

I entered the lobby of a high-rise building and walked toward the elevator to take me to the top-floor restaurant where my former colleagues were gathered. A voice cried out: 'Hey, you, stop!' I presumed that the man behind the building's front desk must have been speaking to someone else. Two of his colleagues emerged from a side room and went straight for me. I explained that I had been out of the country and was unfamiliar with the new normal. Somewhat disbelievingly, they relented, I signed in, produced identification and was allowed to go on my way. Having been in and out of the city's office buildings since I began law school, this was a totally new experience.

While at home, everyone I met up with was keen to hear how things were going in Galway. I was truthful with them; I loved my new position and life in Galway, but of course I had missed Boston and all of them, particularly Karen. I worked hard at teaching and favourable feedback from students suggested that they enjoyed my approach. Karen and I crossed the Atlantic together after two great weeks in Boston and she spent ten days enjoying Ireland. The separation was tough on both of us and we spent a lot of time discussing an uncertain future. At any rate, I dove back into work again and enjoyed another semester in which I took on some committee assignments and further integrated into the life of the law school. In truth, I did so because I wanted to stay longer, despite the travails of a long-distance relationship, and was lucky to extend my fellowship for a second year.

That summer and a second year in Galway passed in a blur and it was decision time. Karen had been a good sport and, if we were going to have a future, it was time for me to come home. I bid a sad farewell to my colleagues, friends and relatives in Galway, vowed to return for a visit as soon as possible and hoped to build on all that I had learned personally and professionally in a rebooted career back in the US. One of my closest friends hit the nail on the head on one of the several 'American wakes' that were held before my departure. 'You're one of us now,' he said. 'You'll be back here to live. Mark my words.' It wasn't what I really wanted to hear, yet deep down, I knew that he was right. At any rate, I had made the decision to leave and I was keen to give America and my relationship a go.

I first moved to Washington, DC in the summer of 2003 and spent every waking hour trying to find suitable employment with little luck. Temporary work back in the law was well-paid, but I couldn't find anything lasting. I had hoped that my experience in Galway and the additional skills I developed there would be a benefit and make me stand out in the crowd. Sadly, recruiters and others I met with didn't see it that way. They were right. It was a terribly frustrating period personally and professionally. I can't have been an easy person to live with. Ultimately, I had to return to Boston, move back in with my parents and begin the search for work there. I soon obtained a position as an independent contractor at a reputable firm. It wasn't exactly what I hoped for, but it paid the bills.

Meanwhile, things weren't working out for Karen and me the way we had anticipated. My disappointment with not being able to find work that I regarded as commensurate with my academic credentials and professional experience was combined with a painful longing for Ireland and the life I had walked away from. I went to Flanagan's Pub in nearby Bethesda, Maryland to watch GAA matches every Sunday and made some friends in the small DC Irish community.

One night etched in my memory is attending the *Veronica Guerin* film with Karen in the cinema in Washington, which was preceded by an advertisement for tourism in Galway, Mayo and Roscommon. I will never forget weeping at the ad when I saw the far-off places and people I had come to love so dearly. Karen and I slowly drifted apart, which I found extremely hard to cope with emotionally. She is a great person. It just wasn't meant to be in the end.

I had changed during the two years in Galway. Leaving to one side a faltering relationship and a failure to get on with what I had presumed would be a seamless resumption of a career, bolstered by another feather in my cap that would set me apart from the rest, there were things about America that I hadn't noticed before, yet were driving me crazy. The tendencies of people to take themselves so very seriously, to obsess over things that don't really matter – like which university they graduated from or the social circle they ran in – and to evaluate those they came across based upon their station in life, however subtly, were stark in my limited time spent back working in the law and interacting with others in that sphere. Even the two years I spent teaching and in scholarly activity at an internationally renowned university were regularly the subject of stupid jokes that revolved around Ireland and its relationship with alcohol.

I saw the world far differently; my perspective was no longer that of an insular, highly educated American for whom a secure, upper-middle-class life was the end all and be all. And I couldn't hide it. Economic and career successes are great, but my short spell in Ireland had taught me that life was something that should be lived and enjoyed, first and foremost. In that vein, I fully adopted the prevalent corollary here: anyone who gets notions about themselves invariably must be taken down a peg or two.

I recall actually laughing out loud in the course of a job interview at a Boston law firm with a lawyer only a few years my senior. It started with boring banter about the academic and sporting rivalries at the third-level institutions we attended and was then followed by a robust, gleefully told tale of how incredibly zealously the firm typically spared no expense and pulled out all of the stops to defend against the most minor, inconsequential personal injury lawsuits. It was, quite frankly, absurd at every level. I walked out the door of the well-appointed office, shaking my head and chuckling at how this self-important blowhard would be regarded in the west of Ireland. There was not a chance I could work there. And I wondered if I would find any career that would make me happy in the US.

The reality is that I had begun to see America through Irish eyes.

In the midst of all this, I discovered in that winter of my discontent that the law school was converting the fellowship I had held into a permanent post. It was the first bit of good news I had heard in what seemed like an eternity. I applied for the job, travelled back to Galway where I reunited with family and friends and prayed fervently that things would go my way. I did a reasonably good interview and was offered the position, which came with a new responsibility for developing clinical legal education at NUI Galway.

Clinical legal education is an American innovation that Professor Gerard Quinn had long wished the law school to embrace. It was an honour to be selected to lead this effort in September of 2004. Clinical legal education, at its heart, is derived from the principle that 'learning by doing' should be an essential component of the training of the future of the legal profession. Just as patients would not select a doctor to perform surgery on them had the surgeon only read about it in textbooks, putative clients expect even newly qualified lawyers to have some practical grounding in their profession. As such, in clinical programmes, law students are exposed to law in the 'real world' in a variety of different models. And optimally, they gain a sense of how the law and legal system serve, or all too often do not serve, individuals and groups on the margins of society.

On returning to Galway, I put a tremendous amount of effort and energy into building upon contacts of my colleagues in the local and national legal community to create opportunities for our students to take on clinical placements for which they would receive academic credit and complement their theoretical understanding with practical knowledge.

Thankfully, numerous firms, entities and individuals embraced the idea of clinical legal education and have facilitated hundreds of our students since the programme's establishment. And our students have acquitted themselves exceptionally well. For many of them, it has been the standout element of their legal education and the kick-off point for successful careers in a wide range of fields. The programme has been recognised nationally and internationally and the fact that the other Irish law schools now are all actively engaged in clinical legal education is to be welcomed. At the same time, I began writing and presenting on my efforts to promote clinical legal education in Ireland.

All in all, in the wake of a depressing year back in the US, it was wonderful to be back in Galway. With friends and family, we picked up right where we left off. Resuming the pastimes I had missed so profoundly – going to my favourite pubs, attending Galway football and hurling matches and escaping to my cousins' houses for relaxing weekends – did my soul good. My parents came to visit for lengthy vacations in 2005 and 2006. Looking back on it, that time we were able to spend together was magical. I had gotten a second chance, and I constantly thanked God for the good fortune.

Not everything was rosy, however. My mother's health and quality of life, which had been in decline since the turn of the century, went downhill very quickly from late in 2006. She lifted herself for my brother's wedding in November of that year, but when I returned home for Christmas, she was clearly struggling physically and mentally. My father, my brother and I were immensely worried about her. Mum's deteriorating condition consumed my thoughts throughout 2007. I was filled with dread that we were losing her and that she was in pain.

Additionally, since Karen's and my break-up, I had reverted to form and enjoyed precious little luck with the opposite sex. There were a couple of brief relationships that fizzled out before they got a chance to take off. And I was again quite lonely in this regard, even as my strong network of friends and family in my new home grew bigger. That was soon to change. 2008 was to prove a momentous year of highs and lows.

CHAPTER 12

Finding Love and a Family

It was Saturday, the 8th of December 2007. I had just returned to Galway from speaking at a conference. I was trying to wrap things up at work and preparing to head back to Boston for Christmas celebrations and to see my ailing mother. The 8th, the Feast of the Immaculate Conception, was her birthday. Hence, in a staunchly Catholic family living in a working-class Glasgow suburb, there was only one choice of name: Mary. In reality, as I thought of her that morning, I wondered whether it would be my mother Mary's last Christmas with us.

I spent the morning in the office trying to tie up loose ends before meeting a couple of friends in town for lunch and a few pints. In keeping with standard operating procedure in Galway, perhaps especially in the month of December, a few turned into a few more and it wasn't long before I was running for a taxi to have a very fast shower at home before venturing out to the Christmas party hosted annually by my friend and colleague who was then the Dean of the School of Law, Professor Donncha O'Connell.

I walked in, a little more jolly and outgoing than usual in the wake of that afternoon's activities, and spoke with colleagues and friends. Donncha had indicated that we would be joined at the get-together by two celebrity guests, RTÉ television journalists Teresa Mannion and Eileen Whelan. As good fortune and the somewhat blurry afterglow of the few drinks we had each consumed would have it, I wound up deep in conversation with Eileen in the kitchen of Donncha's home in Moycullen, County Galway for some time. And downright bizarrely for me, we even wound up slow-dancing in that kitchen. It was an enjoyable night.

Focused as I then was on finishing up at the law school, my impending trip home and my mother's health, I didn't think much about it until I received a forwarded text the following evening to the effect that Eileen had enjoyed my company and would like to see me again. Given her status as one of Ireland's best-known newsreaders, I was hugely flattered by the kind words. It was a nice ego boost I happily shared with my pals in Galway and further afield.

I travelled back to Boston for a Christmas where it never stopped snowing. My mother was better than I had anticipated at first. My father guessed that she had mustered up all that she had and put on a brave face in the knowledge that I was coming home. Nonetheless, I was heartened by her spirit and struck by the extent to which her Scottish accent, dulled from half a century of living in the US, had returned and was stronger than I ever remembered it. She was not the woman she once was, yet at least initially, my impression was that she might have a few years left. Sadly, her condition worsened as I was at home and the grave tone in which friends and relations asked how I thought she was told their own story.

As ever, it was great to see all of the old gang, even though socialising wasn't as frequent or spontaneous as it always had been because more of them had their own young families who had become their first priority. We still knocked a few days and nights out of it at our sorely missed old haunts and at festive house parties. And I was thrilled to receive an email from Eileen – wishing me the best for Christmas and wondering if we could meet up in 2008. The emails went back and forth across the Atlantic for the next ten days and, because I was booked on an overnight flight on New Year's Eve to Dublin, we planned a date in the city on the 1st of January.

It was, of course, incredibly hard to bid my mother farewell. My hope on arrival had dissipated and my concerns were justifiably renewed. I did tell her before I jumped on the MBTA once again to Logan Airport that I had met someone nice on her birthday, as it happened, and that we were getting together the next day. She grasped what I said, wished me the best and told me that she loved me. Neither of us could know it then, but it was the last real conversation we would have on this earth.

I landed in Dublin first thing the next morning and, ahead of our big date, I realised that I had made a huge mistake. Because I had planned to get on a bus straight to Galway from Dublin Airport and had been preoccupied with other things, I had no clean underwear or socks with me. Moreover, Dunnes, Penneys, etc. were all closed on account of the New Year's Day holiday. After checking into a city centre hotel I had booked and having a rest, I went out to see what I could do to remedy the situation.

In the end, the only option was Carroll's Gift Shop in Temple Bar, where I purchased a Guinness t-shirt, Guinness boxer shorts and a pair of socks covered in shamrocks and with an inscription: 'The Leprechauns made me drink it!' I had no idea which way things would go on the night, but over a few pints that afternoon to overcome the sweat-inducing anxiety I was having at the thoughts of a fast-approaching first date with a very attractive Irish household name I barely knew, I made up my mind to bring it up right away and hopefully break the ice in the process.

I finally conjured up the courage to ring Eileen to make a plan. We arranged to meet at the atmospheric Shelbourne Hotel bar for a drink before going for dinner. I was there promptly at the hour we had agreed upon and nervously awaited her arrival. When she eventually turned up, I felt at ease almost instantly. We had a great chat about how our respective Christmases had gone. She laughed wholeheartedly when I showed off my colourful socks and mused out loud as to whether I could persuade her to see the rest of my new wardrobe.

When we went for dinner, Eileen didn't hold back either. She had an eight-year-old son, Seán, who she was raising on her own; was ten years older than me; and lived nearly an hour south in Wicklow Town. She had ample reasons to be a few minutes late. Not even knowing how the date would pan out, none of the revelations frightened me off and I enjoyed hearing more about her life and her enormous family. Eileen is one of 14 children. It was a terrific night and I had a lot to think about on the train journey back to Galway on the second day of 2008. I wanted to see Eileen again and I thought she was on the same wavelength.

I spoke to friends and relations there and back in Boston to see what they thought. Was it a good idea to start a relationship with a woman for whom another little man, Seán, was always going to be the number-one priority? How big a deal was the age difference? What about her living on the other side of the country in a county that hadn't come close to my radar screen when all I really knew and loved about Ireland was the west? I heard a lot of things, but the overarching theme was that I should take it a day at a time and see how things went. In hindsight, these were the proverbial famous last words.

I went to Wicklow for our next date where I first met Seán, who had defied orders and stayed up way too late on a school night to see who was taking his mother away from him. Fortunately, from the very beginning, he was extremely accepting of and welcoming to a stranger who would quickly become a major figure in his life. When we were considering what we might do the next time we met up, Eileen asked me how I would feel about going to Mallorca with her for the weekend to join her at a friend's 40th birthday celebration? I went along and it was great. Our third date was in Spain. Needless to say, things were moving fast.

Shortly after returning, however, I got a phone call with the news I'd been dreading for a while. The outlook was bleak for my mother and I needed to get on a plane. I got there on Saturday, the 2nd of February, and my mother was in a bad way. One didn't need to be a medical professional to recognise that the end wasn't far off. She hung on until the 6th, but when she went, it was a release more than anything else. It was no life for her and she never would have wanted to carry on like that.

As most people who've lost a parent will attest, the support of good friends and family afterward is all that you really have to lean on in the days following an inevitable life event, yet one that is incredibly difficult no matter how well prepared you think you are for it. They all seriously rose to the occasion and couldn't do enough for my dad, my brother and me when we were hurting so badly. It was emotionally wrenching to say goodbye to my bereft father and I was unable to stop the tears from flowing in front of fellow passengers when he dropped me at the T station as I had to get back to work and life in Ireland. Dad visited a lot in the coming months and I managed to convince him to cross the Shannon and to spend a couple of days in Dublin where I organised for him to meet Eileen.

It couldn't wait, because we were already talking about the future in a very serious way. Without saying it explicitly, I was introducing my father to the woman who would soon become his daughter-in-law. When we made it official and got engaged, Dad was initially apprehensive, protective of a son he thought was still in a fragile emotional condition and mightn't be thinking straight. It wasn't long, however, before Eileen won him over. Dad warmed to her swiftly.

When Eileen and I crossed the Atlantic for an engagement party my father hosted at one of our favourite Irish pubs (owned and operated by a Galway man) downtown where almost everyone else was meeting her for the first time, Dad paid Eileen what I still think is a simultaneously simple and extraordinary compliment, coming as it did from an understated man who never did fakeness: 'My wife, Mary, would have loved you. It's such a pity she didn't get to meet you.' My friends of both sexes spoke similarly highly, even as they knew that our marriage doomed the chances of my returning to our shared home turf for anything longer than a vacation.

Our engagement came seven months after we met. And we were married in May of 2009. In addition to Eileen's massive clan, it was fantastic for me to have so many relatives and friends from Boston, Galway and throughout Ireland join in the joyous celebrations. We enjoyed a wonderful honeymoon on Italy's Amalfi Coast and it took the rest of the summer for our feet to get back on the ground. When they did, there were two issues we had to confront as a couple. First was bi-coastal life; my being gone for much of the week was strange for newlyweds. Second was the question of having a child of our own. Neither one was amenable to easy resolution in light of our circumstances.

As for the first, nothing had diminished my appetite for working in academia, for NUI Galway or for the city and county whose people had taken me in as if I were one of their own. At the same time, though, I wondered what it would be like to live full-time at home and to come home to my family every night. It was opportune that a vacancy arose in the Free Legal Advice Centres (FLAC) to lead its Public Interest Law Alliance (PILA). Working as a clinical legal educator in a law school with a strong orientation toward human rights and social justice, I had come to respect and admire FLAC's history of advocacy. Its project, PILA, was focused on expanding the use of law for the public interest through several different strands, one of which was clinical legal education. I decided to apply for the Dublin-based post and was thrilled when it was offered to me on a two-year contract basis. I accepted and was granted a leave of absence from NUI Galway.

It was a privilege to work there for two years with excellent colleagues whose commitment to access to justice for all was unwavering. FLAC's dynamic then director general, Noeline Blackwell, and senior solicitor, Michael Farrell, were just two members of staff whose leadership and energy set the tone for the rest of us. The PILA team concentrated its efforts into convincing more law firms – the large law firms in Dublin particularly – to do *pro bono* legal work in a structured way.

Most firms had always provided legal services for free to individuals and groups in need in an *ad hoc* way. The formalised *pro bono* structure hadn't ever been adopted as it had in the US, UK and elsewhere. Our 'seed planting' and lobbying as to the myriad merits of following the lead of the international firms they were regularly competing with for business and clients yielded results. Now, the vast majority of law firms are doing *pro bono* work and many have signed a pledge that their lawyers will undertake a certain number of *pro bono* hours each year. The victories – large and small – that have been achieved for so many on the margins because of this shift are large in number and diverse in nature. I like to think that PILA has played, and continues to play, a pivotal role in this regard.

While I was in PILA, Eileen and I were struggling to have a child of our own. Like so many couples, it did not come easily. We both wanted to have a son or daughter, but stayed realistic about our chances and steeled ourselves for the prospect that it wouldn't happen. After more than one round of fertility treatment, however, Eileen woke me from my sleep one

Saturday morning in March of 2012 to say that she had taken a test and was pregnant. Stunned and still out of it, I responded incredulously: 'You're what?!' Of course, Eileen had to see her doctor and we had to wait a little while. As soon as we could, though, we spread our wonderful news far and wide.

The toughest person to tell was Seán. How would he react to the fact that he would soon have a sibling? Thankfully, he was his typical easy-going self about it and took the announcement in his stride. At the same time, as we broke the word, there was a lot of planning that needed to be done. It may seem odd, but at Eileen's firm instruction, that included my returning to the law school at NUI Galway – on the other side of the country. Although it had been wonderful to come home every evening, my days at PILA were very long. I left the house every morning at 7 a.m. and didn't get back to Wicklow until around 8 p.m. I would be almost no use to her or to the baby with that schedule, whereas the flexibility of academic life would allow me to be a more actively engaged parent when I was there. I informed my colleagues at both places and prepared for a resumption of my academic career, as well as for fatherhood.

Despite being an older mother-to-be, Eileen had a relatively straightforward and thankfully uneventful pregnancy. She was also very tolerant of my having many 'things will be different from here on' parties in Ireland and the US. Before we knew it, the November day of reckoning was almost upon us. It was still a week or so away when I received a phone call after what was supposed to be a routine check-up. I'll never forget the words Eileen spoke: 'Larry, the baby is coming tomorrow.'

Thoughtlessly, I mumbled something about being busy and having to fulfil a commitment at the university. Realising the ridiculousness of what I had said, I apologised to my wife, made the necessary excuses in Galway and caught the next train to Dublin that evening.

All I can say about the next 24 hours is that Eileen is a lot stronger and braver than I am. There were a few twists and turns in the road, but at the end of it, we were getting acquainted with our son, Lawrence Paul Donnelly IV. He was named for my father. We went home a couple of days later. My most important work – to be a good father – commenced from that moment. To say that Larry Óg changed the dynamic in our house is an understatement of epic proportions. There is no sugar-coating it: parenting a child in his or her early years is really hard and draining work. It can be exasperating at times. Yet it is a labour of love. And it is also striking how quickly one can learn the ropes, even one as generally incompetent as me, when there is no other choice.

Standout moments from those early days include his christening, his first trip – after a long and downright nightmarish six-hour flight preceded by a lengthy delay – to meet his Boston family and friends and his first words and steps. At the time, because it wasn't easy, those days seemed endless. Looking back, they went by in a blur. Larry has developed into a bright, athletic, kind, curious and witty boy. He is the mirror image at the same age of his namesake, my dad. Watching as his personality has developed has been a sheer joy.

Sport is definitely his true love. He has embraced our support for the Boston teams and Galway GAA, as well as his older brother's affinity for Manchester United and for soccer generally, which he plays competitively and with ability that belies his years. And most importantly to me, he inherited his father's passion for golf. He began watching the majors on television before his fourth birthday and prevailed upon me to take out two memberships for us at Wicklow Golf Club. Thanks to Larry, I have gotten back into playing the sport after more than two decades largely away from it. I am enormously grateful to him for this – or at least I am during the rounds in which I am swinging the club well – and cannot wait to see him continue to improve his already gorgeous swing and strong overall game in the future.

Meanwhile, for Eileen and me, it feels like Seán was eight and then almost instantly became a man, such was the way the intervening years flew by. It was a real honour for me to adopt him just before his 18th birthday. As I often say, he is commendably more mature, relaxed and sensible than his adoptive father was in every respect at his age. And Eileen and I, while we have been through an awful lot and are the first to recognise that marriage and parenting aren't always easy, still have a very special bond that, every so often, we manage to rekindle. A trip back to our honeymoon spot, the Amalfi Coast, on the occasion of our 10th wedding anniversary was one such time.

On the down side, Eileen lost her mother in 2015. She had been suffering with dementia and had reached the good age of 89. It wasn't easy for the Whelans when it happened, especially not for my father-in-law, yet ultimately it was for the best given how her quality of life had declined. My father-in-law, meanwhile, is hale and hearty in his early 90s. Prior to the onset of COVID-19, he was delivering meals on wheels, playing bowls and getting out for a few pints. Still, he is undaunted and just keeps going. He provides a valuable example to us all.

Sadly, my own father began to struggle mentally and physically in late 2016 and early 2017. He suffered a terrible fall in 2018 and I rushed back to Boston as the prognosis was extremely grim. I spent more than three weeks with him shuttling back and forth between a rehabilitation centre and area hospitals. When I left him, I was fully certain that I would never see him alive again. The reticence of his doctors and nurses to dispute my lay diagnosis was all the evidence I needed to inform colleagues, family and friends that I would be getting on a plane imminently. I was totally wrong.

To the surprise of virtually everyone, he pushed on and kept going. He was confined to a nursing home, but had frequent visitors – the Donnelly-Whelans of Wicklow included. We wrote to him regularly and prayed that he derived solace from it. When we did get to chat in person or on the phone, it was with great difficulty because of his poor hearing. The typically featured topics were the weather or what time his next meal was being served at. It was a far cry from the non-stop talk about politics, past and present, which formerly consumed our time together to the consternation of others less obsessed with our family's business. How I would have loved to have heard his invariably lucid and insightful take on the long-term ramifications of Donald Trump's presidency or events in Massachusetts politics.

Then, the pandemic struck. With limited visitors and lots of time spent in solitude, the impact was profound. We continued to write to him, but my brother, when pushed, admitted that Dad barely glanced at anything anymore. His communication skills, memory and mobility deteriorated rapidly. He began to develop urinary tract infections. I didn't think much when I heard that he had another one and was spending a few days in the hospital as a result. My brother phoned me shortly thereafter, however, to inform me that his nurses and doctors had noticed a serious change in his condition and that the end was near. I may have known it was coming and was steeling myself on an ongoing basis since 2018, yet it hurt badly. It was even worse when, having considered all of the restrictions and practicalities, I realised that it would not be feasible for me to travel back for the wake and funeral when he passed away. Tommy recorded portions of his visits to our dad in the last days so I could feel like I was there with him. I waved and told him that I loved him, not that he fully understood. Dad was struggling. I prayed that God would take him.

Early in the morning of the 15th of April 2021, Tommy phoned to say that Dad had died. The finality of it hit hard. Naturally, it was devastating not to be there, but technology helped us to participate in the wake, to be virtually present at his beautiful funeral Mass and to see the Korean War-era Army veteran buried with full military honours. As ever, Eileen was an incredible support. Since he passed away, just a couple of weeks shy of his 87th birthday, I've tried to take the big-picture view. He had a good, long life – albeit with a tough period at the finish – and is now reunited with our mother. I have lots of wonderful memories that will never leave me.

We had an amazing bond and I loved him so much. I can say honestly that everything I have ever done in life has been to garner his approval – to make him think that I was living up to the very high expectations he set for me. I hope I have. Selfishly speaking, though, there have been so many moments in recent years where I've wished Dad was at the end of the phone line to offer a quick steer or useful historical background before I went on radio or television. Now that he is gone, I know that I always will.

CHAPTER 13

Back in the Game of Politics

Shortly after I had met Eileen, and by total coincidence, a researcher on RTÉ Radio 1's *Drivetime* programme met up with our mutual friend, my NUI Galway colleague Donncha O'Connell. The race for the Democratic nomination for president was well underway and looked to be an epic battle between the former First Lady and US Senator from New York, Hillary Clinton, and a first-term member of the same body named Barack Obama. The show, hosted at the time by Mary Wilson, was planning to cover the campaign extensively and was seeking a commentator based in Ireland to provide regular analysis of it. Donncha was kind enough to suggest me for the part and I received a call early in 2008 to appear on the programme.

I had never been on anything bigger than local media beforehand and was a nervous wreck for the entire day in the run-up to the phone ringing around 5 p.m. I prepared for every possible question that Mary Wilson, a skilled interviewer, could have put to me. Despite the anxiety, I managed to get through it and acquitted myself reasonably – at least according to Eileen, who was sitting next to me throughout the segment. The buzz and rush of adrenaline

I got from speaking to hundreds of thousands of listeners was something else.

And the programme came back to me repeatedly throughout that topsy-turvy contest until Obama had vanquished Clinton. For me, it was hugely enjoyable and rewarding to sit in the pundit's chair. It was something I had long dreamed of, yet probably would have remained beyond reach if I had remained in the US, where Boston Irish lawyers with a passion for politics and an affiliation to the Democratic Party are more dime a dozen than diamond in the rough. Before long, I was being asked onto other networks and programmes to comment on where I thought that election would head and on what the fallout would be.

It was fascinating to gauge the reaction of the Irish people to the rise of Barack Obama, a transformative figure simply by virtue of being an African-American who was closer to the White House than any other. Most found him inspiring and a welcome antidote following eight years of George W. Bush. The widespread perception here was that the second President Bush had squandered whatever moral authority the US still had by launching an unjustified war against Iraq in the wake of 9/11. He was deemed a bully, and an ignorant one at that by an overwhelming majority here.

Generally speaking, I did not disagree with their assessment. What I found troubling, however, was how often and how seamlessly revulsion at President Bush's misguided foreign policy seemed to either stem from or give rise to anti-Americanism in some quarters. On more than one occasion both in discussions with academics at NUI Galway and in media studios, I had to bite my tongue as nasty, snobbish comments were made about the country of my birth and Americans whose politics weren't necessarily mine, but who I thought were caricatured grossly unfairly. It was a difficult time in many respects for Americans living abroad. If sentiments had reached this nadir in a typically friendly place like Ireland, I can only imagine what those living in less favourably disposed territory experienced.

In this milieu, Barack Obama represented a fresh ray of hope. Bill Clinton is the best instinctive politician of my lifetime. Barack Obama is the most charismatic and inspirational leader of my lifetime. His soaring rhetoric, delivered with the skill and conviction of a fiery pastor, moved people across the ideological spectrum around the world. I was taken with him.

I was particularly enthusiastic about his presidential candidacy because I deeply feared the bellicose attitude of his Republican opponent in 2008, the late John McCain. The tag I usually attached to the war hero and Arizonan – 'He's never seen an international problem for which he doesn't have a military solution' – was rooted in his repeated public pronouncements and his voting track record over decades in the US House and Senate. In the end – partly because McCain was struggling to overcome the Bush legacy, partly because he was running against an extraordinary individual – Obama won the presidency handily. I celebrated his triumph for many reasons, not least of which was that it stood as a direct rebuke to anti-Americans who asserted that our horribly racist nation would never elect a black man.

I continued to comment in the media about the Obama presidency. The administration's Herculean effort to expand access to healthcare for low-income Americans was one element of his tenure that captured popular attention here. Just as most other residents of developed countries, Irish people were broadly aghast that there was such steadfast opposition to the notion that quality healthcare was a right, not a privilege. To his credit, Obama persevered and, even if critics say the ultimate legislative package fell short of what was needed, achieving change was a feat. Observing healthcare politics from afar, it was striking that what sets the US apart, and not in a good way, from Western Europe is the still prevalent 'rugged individualist' ethos and the suspicion that a sense of societal solidarity is a first cousin of socialism.

I also joined Democrats Abroad Ireland and became its legal counsel. I met some great people through the organisation, all of whom had their own fascinating stories to tell about how they wound up in Ireland. In truth, many members of DA-Ireland do not stand out as Americans because they are actually Irish emigrants who became US citizens, yet returned home to live after a period of time there. I remain very proud of our efforts to engage American citizens and to encourage them to exercise their sacred right to vote which they retain, no matter how long they have been away. Naturally, given that my own politics are decidedly centrist, my guess is that fellow activists in the organisation would have disagreed vehemently with me on myriad issues, but there was much that united us.

One of those things was opposition to the former Governor of Massachusetts, Mitt Romney, who ran against President Obama in 2012. His comment to supporters during the campaign revealed a bias against the less well-off; people who had not been born into tremendous privilege as he had: 'There are 47 percent of the people who will vote for the president no matter what' because they are 'dependent upon government … believe they are victims … believe the government has a responsibility to care for them … these are people who pay no income tax.' It infuriated me and I can't say that I hid my disdain for the ex-governor of my home state in my media commentary that year. Fortunately, Obama cruised to a second term.

And the real highlight for me of that period was that Larry Óg had been born just a couple of days previously. Indeed, his birth became national news several days later when a researcher on the late Marian Finucane's Sunday morning radio programme on which I was a panellist dashed into the studio with a piece of paper. Marian, in typically warm and eloquent fashion, told the country that I had more than one reason to be exhausted 'by the arrival of another Larry Donnelly into the world, just in time for the election and with the political gene no doubt'.

In the summer of 2011, I was approached by Niall O'Dowd – who had considered a bid for the Irish presidency earlier that year and who I had advised as he explored what would have been a longshot, but in my view compelling, candidacy – to do some writing for his Irish-American news website, IrishCentral.com. I used the platform he afforded me to inform the diaspora about politics and current affairs in an Ireland they have varying levels of connection to, to offer an 'outside looking in' perspective on what was happening stateside and to dispute what I regard as a defeatist and misguided school of thinking about the declining vitality of Irish-America. It gave me a taste for 'columnising' and the often vitriolic ripostes contained in the comments section helped to thicken my skin.

Subsequently, I began writing for TheJournal.ie, which I believe to be the country's most innovative news source and which regularly features some of Ireland's best journalism. Because there is no subscription fee, it reaches people that other publications do not. Being a TheJournal columnist remains a great privilege to the present day. While my early media commentary on American politics was quite stridently pro-Democrat, I deliberately resolved to provide a more balanced point of view shortly after the re-election of Barack Obama. This is probably most evident in my pieces for TheJournal.

To a great extent, this conscious decision was driven by what I think is the fairly obvious bias in media organs outside of the US against the Republican Party and conservatives generally. To me, the public is not well served by what sometimes can be a one-sided narrative that declines to give the other point of view a fair hearing or to understand why so many Americans lean to the right. It is perhaps because I am a Democrat who is also a practising Catholic and thinks that the party has veered too far to the left on cultural issues that this shift has come quite naturally. Either way, I find it amusing that social media commentators responding to what I have said or written alternatively say that I am a total shill for the Democrats, on the one hand, or a closet backer of the GOP, on the other.

I was extremely flattered when my more nuanced media punditry caught the eye of the late *Irish Times* columnist and senior counsel, Noel Whelan. As its founder, he invited me to speak at the first Kennedy Summer School in New Ross, County Wexford in 2012 and at each summer school that followed until he asked if I would get involved in organising it and serve as co-director. I believe that Noel was the premier Irish political commentator of the first part of this century whose media contributions warranted silence, attention and reflection, such was their merit. It was a privilege to work with Noel for several years on the Kennedy Summer School, as well as on a successful effort to avoid the abolition of Seanad Éireann in a 2013 referendum. Noel was a masterful political strategist and it was in that and subsequent referendums on marriage equality and the repeal of the 8th Amendment prohibition on abortion that he had his most significant impact.

Through the Kennedy Summer School, I have had the opportunity to interview and get to know at a personal level major figures like *New York Times* columnist Maureen Dowd, conservative commentator Cal Thomas, former US Congressman Bruce Morrison, RTÉ's former Washington Correspondent Caitríona Perry and a litany of others. Perhaps even more importantly, I have become close friends with the other members of the organising committee of the summer school and found yet another Irish home base among the proud residents of the wonderful town of New Ross. I was on a Kennedy Summer School trip to Boston in April of 2019 with Noel when he discovered that he was seriously unwell. Sadly, the illness progressed swiftly and he passed away in July. It shook all of us on the summer school team, but we carried on because we knew how badly Noel would have wanted us to and we will continue to carry on with what has become a fixture on the Irish and American political calendars every September.

The Kennedy Summer School, similar to every other outlet for discourse on American life, was virtually taken over by the unexpected ascendancy of Donald Trump all the way to the White House. For my own part, much of what I have done since the political earthquake that was his election in 2016 has been to seek to explain how and why he won. Speaking despairingly to Eileen before appearing on RTÉ Radio 1's *Morning Ireland* at 6 a.m. on the Wednesday after he defeated Hillary Clinton, she offered one small comfort: 'I know you're terribly disappointed, but this will be the best thing that has ever happened to your media career.'

And she was right. The Irish people, who have always had a huge interest in the politics of a country they have such a strong connection to, looked on avidly with a mixture of disbelief and horror at the behaviour of a truly unprecedented leader of the Western world. I'd be lying if I said that I was not surprised by Trump's election. At the same time, however, I understood it. The 21-year-old Larry Donnelly was an ardent backer of Trumpism – insofar as it represents a blend of social conservatism and America First insularity – and would probably have looked past his significant personal failings and voted for him over Hillary Clinton for a variety of reasons. Because this was once in me, I get it. And from the ruthlessly agnostic perspective of a political strategist, I have long thought this was the winning formula for the Republican Party – that President George HW Bush may have thwarted Pat Buchanan's primary challenge in 1992, but that, in an era transformed by globalisation, technology and more, Buchanan's progeny (which is who Trump is, even though he loathes Buchanan!) could eventually win the battle for the heart and soul of a conservative movement that would attract a new and once implausible coalition of followers. There is a way to go, yet it's difficult to dispute the fact that the Republicans in 2021 are where I was in the early 1990s.

In any case, that's my back story: how my family, like so many other Irish emigrants who came before and after them found a land of opportunity in the US, in Boston specifically, and rapidly climbed the ladder in the worlds of politics, academia, the professions and more; the ways in which a distinctly Boston, Irish and Catholic upbringing and education formed me, together with my personal and professional development; how my own political creed drifted gradually from the hard right to the centre; and how I opted to make an unusual journey back across the Atlantic to a place that has been my land of opportunity, both personally in my family life and professionally in my two-pronged career.

It's been a really enjoyable and never boring journey that has equipped me with a relatively unique perspective on the two countries that are my home. I am an American and a proud Boston area native to the core. But I have spent the bulk of my adult life in Ireland and see the world through Irish eyes also. There are many who've gone the opposite direction; there are few who travelled the same direction as me, and fewer still who've embraced their ancestral Ireland as their own country to the extent I have.

Part Three – The View from the Centre

CHAPTER 14

A Cultural and Political Re-education

One might say that it's easy to move to a new country that you have visited before many times, where you have family and friends and where they speak the same language. And all things considered, it surely is. Nonetheless, there was a lot for a 26-year-old, parochial Bostonian to absorb on coming 'home' to Ireland. There was a process of adjustment; it could be said that it continues to this day. The immersion, used to generate hot water in the house, for instance, is something I will never fully get to grips with. There are plenty of other things that fall into the category of unsolvable mysteries.

I was only in Galway for a couple of weeks when a housemate instructed me that a towel could be retrieved from the 'hot press' in the event that I needed one. Before asking for clarification on the point, I wondered to myself, what on earth is a hot press? I soon discovered that a hot press was what I would always have known as a closet, whereas an ordinary 'press' was what I would call a cabinet. Shortly thereafter, I learned that Hoover had totally cornered the market on vacuum cleaners and had actually been turned into a verb: 'hoovering' instead of 'vacuuming' was the label for that horrible household chore. And this was merely the beginning of this Yankee's acculturation.

On one of my first forays for lunch in Galway, I received a stark reminder that I wasn't in Boston anymore. As a law student and then practising lawyer, every morning, I anticipated choosing from a wide array of delicious, heaped, hot and cold sandwiches from the superb delis that dot the downtown area. On offer now were a limited variety of miserable, underwhelming sandwiches with one slice of meat, a grossly disproportionate amount of bread and a vile combination of butter and mayonnaise. To say it was a let-down is a colossal understatement. Moreover, at pubs and restaurants, there was the ice famine. My understanding had been that a glass of ice was just that, a glass of ice. In Galway, it turned out to be two or three measly, half-melted cubes at the bottom. I don't get it. Ice is free, after all. We Americans like our drinks cold – and no, they can never be too cold.

Irish people tend to prefer hot drinks in my experience, with tea at the top of the list. Before arriving here, I never understood just how much the Irish love their tea. Obsession is not too powerful a word. I have heard more 'Barry's vs Lyons' debates over the years than I care to recall. And for a substantial segment of the population, events in life – whether sad or joyous, work or pleasure – revolve around cups of tea. There is nothing at all wrong with this. It's actually quite nice, surely comforting and totally harmless. Yet tea doesn't do it for me at all. I would almost always prefer something colder or, to my shame, stronger, than a cup of tea.

The conversations that invariably flow over cups of tea highlight another major cultural distinction between my two homes. I frequently find myself straining to hear Irish people who tend to speak softly, even when in crowded places. While I rarely say 'Huh?' – or 'haaah' in Boston parlance – in America, I constantly say it here, to the annoyance of my wife and others. There is no doubt that we have a tendency to be loud. Memorably, the owner of an establishment in Waterville, County Kerry once erected a sign banning 'loud Americans' from the premises. Although the proprietor was foolish to turn away potentially deep-pocketed customers, I concede that he has a point. I witness it when my friends and family come over to visit. Generally, they are louder. Conversely, I don't wish Irish people were as loud and brash as my fellow Americans, but I do regularly wish they would speak up.

Of course, this stuff is fairly trifling in the grand scheme of things and has been well-chronicled in some instances. The world would be quite dull if we were all the same. What I love about Ireland vastly outweighs the aspects of living here that I find annoying. I wouldn't be here otherwise.

Beyond the mundane, there are major differences in the two things that move me above all – politics and religion – that have taken some getting used to. As is nearly always the case, neither place has it 100% right.

Back in Boston, I had found the increasing zeal with which some advocates wanted religion banished altogether from sight both sad and pathetic. I cannot fathom how or why the public expression of religious faith, practise and belief is considered out of bounds or even offensive. With the possible exception of some radical sects, the central tenets usually revolve around love, respect and a hope that there is something more and better than this life. Attempts to ban symbols like a crucifix or menorah from government-owned buildings or land baffle me. I have never met anyone of another faith or none who felt persecuted or diminished by their presence. And I have no time for the radicals, some of whom have been centrally involved in the successful effort to push my Democratic Party to the extreme cultural left, for whom this initiative is an animating impulse. Maybe as a response to the rise of secularism, there are religious people – primarily Catholics, in fact – who seem to look for offence and to overplay the degree to which their faith now makes them societal pariahs. I don't have much time for these people either. Furthermore, the hypocrisy of many evangelical Christians is similarly off-putting.

Prior to relocating, because I had spent time there as a child and a young adult and was acquainted with the attitudes of relations and friends, I knew well that 'Catholic Ireland' had been relegated to the past, despite the image some less connected Irish-Americans stubbornly clung to. And given the horrific things that were done by an institution that held absolute power for far too long, the dethroning of Catholicism was entirely appropriate and long overdue. But I was heartened that religion and religiosity hadn't been pushed out of the public arena altogether. Nonetheless, I was struck by how few people of my own age still attended Mass weekly. Hardly anyone I met went and I was typically looked at oddly when I indicated that I tried not to miss Mass on Sundays and went during the week when time permitted. Indeed, many vociferously rejected the Church in the wake of their own less-than-ideal childhood experiences of it.

And I have certainly heard some rather harrowing stories about what was done, purportedly in the Church's name. Probably because I didn't want to believe it, I found these pained recollections both surprising and sickening. I don't blame those who endured misdeeds at the hands of those who held a sacred trust for leaving. That said, much of the population continues to desire the institution to be a part of the key events of their lives: birth, marriage and death. Additionally, First Holy Communion is still a rite of passage for many children whose parents long ago abandoned Catholicism.

So, while the Boston Irish are defined in many respects to this day by their Catholicism and many, such as my own family and lots of our friends, celebrate it in robust defiance of a secular society, there is an ever-shrinking pool of similarly observant Catholics in Ireland and a far bigger cohort who could correctly be described as agnostic about their Catholicism, except on specific occasions. In short, here there has been a break from the Church, yet it is not a clean break. It's complicated – and the tension in the relationship between the Church and the people it formerly claimed as its disciples has increasingly come to the fore in Irish politics.

And learning about the politics of my new home was an urgent priority in my first months in Ireland. It was a nerd's dream come true. I began with some simple online searches about the Irish political system. I devoured the political content of the broadsheet newspapers in an effort to inform myself as to what was then transpiring. I spoke to and asked a battery of surely irritating, very basic questions of everyone I came across who was involved in politics at any level. I read a number of books about Irish politics – Stephen Collins' *Breaking the Mould: How the PDs Changed Irish Politics* is one that stands out – to get a basic grounding in the historical background. Fortunately, from my perspective, there was a general election in the spring of 2002.

I used that election and the campaign that preceded it as a crash course in the nitty-gritty of Irish politics. That was the first election I cast a vote in as an Irish citizen in the Galway West constituency. I still recall the dumbfounded look on the face of the poll worker that afternoon in May when I provided my name and address (across from Pearse Stadium where I was residing) in an accent which announced that it was a long way from Galway City's Salthill suburb that I had grown up. On the day of the count, I happened to be at a party in County Leitrim with my cousin John. The RTÉ coverage was on a television in a side room, well away from where people were mingling. Immediately upon noticing it, I strolled over, took a seat on the couch and was so riveted that I declined to get up from it and rejoin the gathering. I wished my dad was sitting beside me.

There were obviously a number of substantial differences between the politics that I had grown up in and around and Irish politics. It took some time to figure out proportional representation and get used to ranking candidates in order of preference, as opposed to simply putting an 'X' next to the candidate I favoured. Having a wealth of choices, not just Republican or Democrat, in terms of parties was a further mystery to unravel. A clear advantage of the range of choice, as well as multi-seat constituencies, means that those who are elected are more broadly representative of the people they serve. Whereas in the US, many voters loathe or are actually ashamed by the winning person in a two-candidate race who may have been elected by a slim majority to take a seat. It could be argued that the aversion that clearly arises helps drive the apathy and anger which translate into the US having one of the lowest rates of voter participation of the world's representative democracies.

. These multi-seat constituencies, which can engender even more bitter intra-party than inter-party battling and dirty tricks, were another new wrinkle. How does Dáil Éireann operate? What is a TD and how is that role similar to and different than that of a member of the US Congress or, more appropriately, of a state legislator? What is Seanad Éireann and does it remotely resemble the upper houses at the federal or state level in America? A key distinction in this regard is that there is a brightly defined delineation between the duties and job specifications of elected officials at the federal, state and local levels in the US. In most instances, even where politicians are from different parties, they have decent working relationships when it comes to constituent services. It is in their interests to do so and they do not hesitate to refer those who seek help elsewhere, depending on what it is that is requested.

In Ireland, though, legislators who should be dealing with national issues are often called upon to deal with things not a million miles away from what I handled as an elected Town Meeting Representative from Precinct 6 in East Milton. And those who do so most diligently and efficaciously commonly get re-elected by significant margins. To be blunt, this is crazy, and it points to the desperate need to empower local government to address everyday problems, while letting TDs and senators focus on the bigger picture.

Lastly, there was trying to ascertain the respective identities and ideologies of the various political parties. The only ones I had any familiarity with in Boston were Sinn Féin, owing to its association with the Irish Republican Army, and Fianna Fáil, largely because they were ordinarily the party of government and would have been featured in the Irish-American media. Its leading politicians and supporters had also been close contacts and friends of my Uncle Brian during the 1980s and early 1990s. I quickly came to understand that Fine Gael were their arch-rivals and the second-largest party. The smaller Labour Party was to the left; the Progressive Democrats were to the right, economically at least; and the Greens were the environmentalists. I was also fascinated by the peculiar creature that is the independent politician in Ireland, especially those who are constituency or single-issue oriented.

What I was most perplexed by in those early days was that Irish politics was not defined by ideological combat. Notwithstanding what I think are the rather bizarre protestations of people outside the US that there are no significant policy differences between Democrats and Republicans, the two parties take opposing stances in their platforms on a host of cultural, economic and foreign policy subjects. Following the decline of political centrism, they really couldn't be more different. With that as personal experience, there was one question

I asked repeatedly of political types: 'What is the difference between Fianna Fáil and Fine Gael?' My own take was that they were indistinguishably centrist in their orientation. Most of the answers focused on historical and cultural, rather than philosophical, divergence. Historically, Fianna Fáil opposed the Anglo-Irish Treaty, while Fine Gael backed it. Culturally, Fianna Fáil was the party of traditional nationalism, the Irish language, devotees of the Gaelic Athletic Association, small farmers and much of the working class. Fine Gael supporters, on the other hand, were less republican-leaning, more likely to be wealthy, to be professional people or large landowners and to be rugby fans or golfers. These responses, invariably shaped by the biases of those who shared them, were sweeping generalisations, yet they were not without a kernel of truth to them. But the prejudices reflected in them shed precious little light on the differences between them on the issues that matter.

It has been posited in the past by politicians and pundits of all stripes that there actually is no discernible ideological difference between the two moderate entities. It possibly can be contended that Fianna Fáil is more left economically and right socially than Fine Gael, but this may be the equivalent of a rule with so many exceptions to it that it is meaningless in practice. Coming from a country with a pronounced and ever-sharpening right vs left political divide, it was difficult to comprehend that a party's culture, as well as its stance on a treaty in a turbulent civil war period many decades previously, could so define it in the hearts and minds of the citizenry in the early twenty-first century. Yet dozens of conversations with activists from both camps demonstrated that it did.

From spending most of my time in the west with precious few trips across the Shannon, I learned quickly that, if there was a divide in Ireland, it was between Dublin and the rest of the country. That divide operates at myriad levels, yet seems quite easily exploitable in politics. For a rural politician, the words 'up above in Dublin' are extremely potent. Their constituents can and do read a huge amount into it. That's where all the money and investment goes. That's where the infrastructure is. Part of it is full of rich snobs; part of it is inhabited by criminals and lowlifes. We live in the real Ireland; Dublin isn't the real Ireland. Both in jocular and not so jocular language, any visitor who has spoken to Irish people outside the capital will have heard these sentiments expressed. Indeed, many friends in Boston whose families come from the west have still never visited Dublin, having been warned off it by their cousins. My own family and friends in Galway aren't exactly enamoured of the city and its hinterlands where nearly half the population of Ireland resides by some estimates.

It is a fact that a substantial percentage of Dublin residents have roots elsewhere and that many young people growing up in rural Ireland aspire to careers in Dublin and ultimately pursue their dreams in the 'big smoke'. Yet as I conducted my outsider's assessment of Irish politics, I often wondered why the Dublin vs the rest of the country fault line wasn't a bigger factor in the character of the parties. In a sense, it would seem far more straightforward to have a grouping that consistently fought for the interests of rural people and areas and another that sought to maintain the position of Dublin. Very strong arguments, with certain concessions and expeditious accommodations, can be made on both sides. And after all, as the political scientist Harold Lasswell proffered, politics is about 'who gets what, when, how'. Lasswell's proposition is a crucial component of the decision-making process for voters in this country and perceptions on this front are relatively easy for skilled politicians to shape and manipulate. Independent TDs who rely on this appeal have been very successful.

For myriad reasons, though, the country is fortunate that its party politics didn't devolve into a clash between urban and rural citizens. The perils of going down that track are manifest in the polarisation in the US – where the Republican Party dominates sparsely populated 'flyover territory' and Democrats run the cities. It is unhealthy for and potentially threatening to the polity. Having to take into account the fortunes of a cross-section of people from diverse backgrounds has probably helped Ireland avoid the extremism that has crept in across Europe and further afield. Ireland may be small geographically, yet its character and people are very different. When parties and groupings seek to enlist adherents from bustling cities, small towns and rural areas alike, they cannot be seen to dramatically favour the interests of one segment of the population over another. Every overture in one direction has to be offset by a gesture to another. This is evident in the measured, cautious approach to contentious topics, such as climate change, housing, healthcare and more. Naturally, this has elicited strong criticism from activists and non-governmental organisations, but it militates strongly against lurches to the right or the left.

If there is one thing American politicians could take from their counterparts in Ireland, for me it would be the less frenetic and charged ambiance around it. There are naturally areas of passionate disagreement and it can get personal occasionally. The atmosphere around Irish politics is much less fraught than in a hyper-partisan US in 2021. By way of example, even the response to COVID-19 in the US deteriorated into squabbling between Republicans and Democrats. The wearing of masks or the reopening of business should have been dictated by public health and safety, not by arguments about freedoms or market theory. There may have been differences of opinion which bubbled over, yet politicians here, in the main, did not flagrantly disregard the advice of experts as many American officeholders proudly did while attributing hard-to-defend stances to ideology or religious faith and a consequent scepticism about science.

Although a politics that is overly dominated by rigid ideological splits, as it is in the US, is prone to fail, one of the attractive aspects of American politics is that, at its best, it can be a marketplace of big ideas. For instance, to draw from right-wing intellectualism, Newt Gingrich's 'Contract with America' in 1994 – after 40 years of Democratic control of the House of Representatives, it was a Republican blueprint for shrinking government, lowering taxes, promoting entrepreneurship, eliminating many social welfare protections and more – was arguably a quite radical reframing of democracy and of the relationship between those elected to office and the people they serve. I do believe strongly in the moderation and incrementalism that still lie at the heart of the Irish political process. That said, I would like to see more big ideas emanating from parties and individuals. The small number of outsiders or almost accidental politicians in Ireland, who have achieved some prominence in other arenas and are less encumbered by convention, could contribute greatly in this regard. It is a pity that a rather hierarchical system – in particular, the operation of the party whip – militates against the open discussion and debate of big ideas from newcomers with useful specialisms and experience.

CHAPTER 15

Reforming Irish Politics

From the moment I figured out the fashion in which an Irish political party works, it has irked me profoundly. In the US, it has been the case for so long that there are merely two major political parties that most of us have come to accept this reality unthinkingly. In truth, it is downright bizarre that there are only two parties to represent approximately 330,000,000 citizens who are diverse in every conceivable way. Historically – though to a lesser extent now than ever – they endeavoured to be big tents who welcomed people who may have had a range of views on specific issues, yet coalesced around some fundamental, overarching principles. Democrats and Republicans have traditionally been rather loose groupings who tolerated dissent from elected officials on matters of import to their disparate constituencies or on so-called issues of conscience.

I knew that their counterparts in multi-party jurisdictions operated rather differently and were more tight-knit collectives where a greater degree of discipline was expected. I was not aware, though, that Irish political parties were so extreme in this regard. It has engendered what I believe to be a profound systemic deficiency in this country's governance. That is the extraordinary power imbalance between the individual politician and the political party he belongs to. It is grossly out of whack. It should be a fundamental tenet of democracy that candidates for political office, once elected, will remain true to themselves and to those who placed their trust in them. It is far more likely, however, that the elected representative in Ireland will follow – whether blindly or not, it doesn't really matter – the dictates of their political party.

TDs are often criticised for engaging in clientelist politics in service of their constituents, but in their defence, that is typically their best opportunity to act as individual public servants, not simply as party apparatchiks. Surprisingly to me, this issue of balance is seldom addressed, though the legendary columnist and broadcaster Vincent Browne did vent at times about the power of the party whip. The late Noel Whelan raised the issue on several occasions and termed moves away from a rigid whip a 'maturing development in Irish politics'. To me, their analysis is axiomatic. But the stringent whip system is broadly accepted as a necessary evil or even robustly defended. I cannot fathom why.

The consideration of a question once posed to me at a university debate – in what were headier times for the US shortly after President Obama's election – crystallises the magnitude of this problem: 'Could there be an Irish Obama?' The answer, simply stated, is no.

First off, if the Illinois Democratic Party chose its nominees for office in the same fashion as an Irish political party, Barack Obama never would have been elected to the United States Senate in 2004. A black, reform-minded, relatively unknown liberal from Chicago would almost certainly have been adjudged too risky a proposition. A moderate Democrat from the 'Chicago machine' or from the conservative southern part of the state would have been considered a more viable candidate and thus ordained the nominee by the party insiders who control the nomination process in Ireland. But an open nomination process in Illinois allowed Obama to take his message to the wider electorate and he cruised to victories in the Democratic primary and general election.

While in office, Senator Obama would have been expected to keep his head down and toe the party line if he were an ambitious young member of an Irish political party. He didn't and, risking the wrath of many senior Democrats in the Senate, lambasted the bi-partisan majority that gave President George W. Bush unbridled authority to wage wars in Iraq and Afghanistan. His stance defined his presidential candidacy and swayed many on the left wing of his party to support him instead of the presumptive nominee, Hillary Clinton. Whatever one's view of President Barack Obama's politics or take on the merit of his presidency, the foregoing are unassailable facts.

Under the status quo in Ireland, an elected official's own beliefs, conscience and free will are subjugated to their party's dictates. With some notable exceptions, the politicians who advance into leadership positions get there because they have demonstrated relentless fidelity to their party above all else and an aptitude for defending the party leadership from attack, even when objectively indefensible. Someone who emulated Barack Obama's fearless approach would have been *persona non grata*. As such, many Irish politicians are compromised by the time they get anywhere near the top. It is no wonder then that the electorate is so cynical about its political leaders.

Irish political parties do sometimes allow TDs to vote their conscience without fear of the party whip. These are so-called 'free votes'. TDs should be allowed to vote their conscience more often, especially on complex moral issues on which people of every stripe may have very strong convictions one way or the other, such as abortion. While some might argue that this would cause legislative paralysis and/or chronic instability, a politician joins a party – at least one would hope – because they generally agree with its ideology, ethos and culture. Consequently, they are likely to support the party on most votes anyway. This is particularly so on close votes on which the fate of a government might hinge.

Of course, party dictates can also prove extremely troublesome on less lofty, more parochial, but every bit as politically volatile, local issues. Whether it's a government decision to close a rail station or withdraw a regional hospital's patient services, voters invariably – and quite justifiably in my view – want the people they put into office to fight for them. Government TDs are all too often put in an impossible position: support the will of their constituents and be ostracised by the parliamentary party or genuflect to party headquarters and face a perilous re-election campaign.

Those who call the shots at party headquarters should reflect on the dilemma they force office holders into and ask themselves a simpler question. Do they want to keep their TD, who supports the party 90% of the time, or to facilitate the election of another aspirant to office, who'll support their agenda virtually none of the time? In the United States, the Democratic and Republican parties, while not encouraging dissent, have said yes to the former and no to the latter. Doing so has allowed each party to elect candidates in ordinarily unfavourable territory. By way of example, there is a very powerful Democratic member of the US Senate from West Virginia, Joe Manchin, and a Democratic governor of the state of Louisiana, John Bel Edwards. The party would have next to no chance of electing a devout progressive state-wide in either of these deep-red strongholds. Senator Manchin and Governor Bel Edwards, however, are well to the right of the Democratic platform on abortion, gun ownership and environmental topics. By forsaking ideological purity, their party gets two more allies on healthcare access, public education, workers' rights and more than they would have otherwise.

My calls to readjust the relationship between the individual and the party have regularly been dismissed as radical and implausible, especially given that they emanate from an outsider whose view is undeniably shaped by long exposure to the far from perfect and not always democratic process in the United States. It would not be a panacea, but I think it would prove an apt, intellectually honest and most interesting reform of Irish politics. Regrettably, I've seen little indication that the parties will change the way they do business anytime soon.

Meanwhile, there is Seanad Éireann, the upper house of the Oireachtas. It has been the subject of considerable discussion and debate over the years. Much of the discourse, unfortunately in my view, has been shaped equally by the scorn and cynicism shared by many political insiders about this legislative body and by the widespread ignorance about and indifference to the Seanad among the Irish people. While these sentiments are lamentable, they are understandable. The journalists who cover Leinster House recognise that it has become something of a developmental league for aspiring TDs and a retirement home for politicians who may best be described as forgotten, but not gone. Ordinary citizens – the overwhelming majority of whom do not get to vote for senators – cannot comprehend the labyrinthine system of elections and appointments through which its 60 members are selected to take their seats.

There have been proposals for reform in the past. Some amounted to tinkering around the edges. For instance, six of the Seanad seats are reserved for graduates of Trinity College Dublin and the National University of Ireland. A 1979 referendum passed by the electorate would have extended the franchise to other graduates of third-level institutions. It was not acted on. Decades later, in what was an attempt to seize a moment when the people were angry at politicians and disgusted with the system in the wake of a terrible recession, a banking crisis and the 2010 International Monetary Fund bailout of Ireland, then-Taoiseach Enda Kenny decided that the country had 'too many politicians for its size' and advocated the abolition of the Seanad in an autumn 2013 referendum. One of the slogans in the ensuing campaign adopted by Kenny's Fine Gael party – 'Fewer Politicians' – was a sad, naked, lowest-common-denominator attempt to appeal to people's worst instincts in a difficult period.

Because I believe so strongly in politics and that most politicians become involved in what is a tough and usually thankless business out of love for their country and community, I was outraged. And I decided to become involved. Thankfully, a group calling itself Democracy Matters, which included stalwarts such as the late Senator Feargal Quinn, LGBT campaigner and later government minister Katherine Zappone, the former Tánaiste and Attorney General Michael McDowell and my friend Noel Whelan, came together to fight this populist initiative. They recognised that defending the Seanad as it was would not cut it; the campaign would have to focus on reforming and reimagining an institution that could not withstand scrutiny as it was then constituted. And they came up with an exciting package of ideas.

Among these were votes for all Irish citizens; giving a say to those in Northern Ireland and to Irish citizens around the globe; and 50/50 gender parity in the body. Democracy Matters also attacked the notions that cost savings would be achieved by eliminating the Seanad or that fewer politicians was actually a good thing, noting the litany of extraordinary figures in Irish history whose voices mightn't have been heard were it not for their winning election to the upper house of the Oireachtas. Additionally, a Seanad could attract a different type of candidate and facilitate the participation of a broader cross-section of society in governance. Lastly, it stressed the potential dangers inherent in getting rid of a second house of the legislature, thereby giving a government the untrammelled capacity to push through its agenda without any checks and balances or braking mechanism – even if the Seanad's powers are limited in this regard, it could still play an important role in the lawmaking process. This final point was crucial in my mind, given that I am very much in favour of bicameral legislatures generally and fear the tyranny of the majority that could arise in a unicameral legislature dominated by a ridiculously over-rigid party whip.

I used whatever media platforms I had to expand upon the central points made by Democracy Matters. I also did some canvassing on Shop Street in Galway for a vote against abolition. This experience did reveal that some members of the public were extremely angry at politicians after a recession that took such an awful toll on them financially and personally. One older man ripped up a leaflet I handed him before screaming a series of epithets about the people in power who had ruined the country. It wasn't pleasant, but I understood his rage and it brought me back to the day when I knocked on the door of the man who dressed me down when I was first seeking election as a Milton Town Meeting Representative years before. In the closing weeks of the campaign, the opinion polls showed the pro-abolition, Yes side with a roughly 60%–40% advantage. A lot of us didn't believe that these polls were accurate, yet still feared that a game changer was required in order to save the Seanad.

Although we didn't get the game changer, we stayed on message. And on the day, we won it by a narrow 52% to 48% margin. It came as a surprise to most observers. As Enda Kenny, who had declined to participate in a televised debate in the run-up said about the result, 'Sometimes in politics you get a wallop.' As well as buying into the arguments posed by Democracy Matters and others, I think that some of the No vote can be attributed to people who wanted to give the government a kick for a variety of unrelated reasons. At any rate, it was wonderful to be a part of a group who stood up to what was a populist, anti-politics and in many ways contemptuous effort to kill off an organ of the state. It looked like a sure thing in the circumstances. But they were defeated.

In the aftermath, we all pledged to keep the heat on to ensure that reform proposals were taken seriously, advanced and implemented as expeditiously as possible. Sadly, this has not transpired. The exciting alterations to how senators would be elected and to how the body could operate have not been acted upon since the Seanad was retained in 2013. This has demonstrated just how resistant to change institutions can be, as well as an attitude to the effect that 'the fools voted to keep it; we'll keep it as a rotten borough' which I believe exists in certain, highly influential quarters. Michael McDowell, now a senator himself, has sought to keep the pressure on and has been a steadfast advocate for necessary reforms. He deserves enormous credit for swimming against the current. I still believe that Seanad Éireann has tremendous, potentially transformative potential – that it could help Irish democracy to go beyond functioning to flourishing if anything resembling the vision Democracy Matters had for it came to be. Hope springs eternal on this front.

Finally, on the subject of political reform, the role in recent years of the citizens' assembly is eminently deserving of mention. The driving forces behind its creation were Professor David Farrell of University College Dublin and Dr Jane Suiter of Dublin City University. The assembly was intended to bring people 'into the heart of debates over constitutional and political reforms to improve how our representative system of democracy operates'. Its initial incarnation was as a Convention on the Constitution in 2012 and a later body called the Irish Citizens' Assembly in 2016. In 2012 and 2016, these gatherings largely did what they said they would: citizens were selected at random who then agreed to give up a series of weekends to hear from experts, deliberate a number of complex issues and, at the close, take votes on what the most appropriate legislative or other solution might be. It has been mooted – and it strikes me as an inspired suggestion – that a citizens' assembly should be established in future to consider the appropriate path for and myriad implications of the potential reunification of the two jurisdictions on this island.

The Convention on the Constitution and the Irish Citizens' Assembly were criticised by those who asserted that the country already had an entity with the constitutional imprimatur to access the best available information, take decisions and make laws – the Oireachtas – and politicians were using the citizens' assembly cynically to avoid tackling contentious and divisive issues, such as same-sex marriage. They might have had a point, yet that does not diminish the reality that this initiative, looked at in an overarching sense, was a success insofar as it engaged citizens, in the classical sense of that word, who surely brought their experience back to their communities.

Moreover, when the votes were cast, it produced multiple surprising results on issues that the politicians had shied away from. Many pundits – yours truly was one – were deeply suspicious of some of the conclusions that these active citizens reached in the particular context they were arrived at. When it came to where the country was on social change, however, we were incorrect. As a matter of fact, we were more than just incorrect – we were dead wrong.

CHAPTER 16

Social Change and Politics

When I began working with the Public Interest Law Alliance in 2010, one of the first events I attended was a gala lunch at the Mansion House in Dublin in support of marriage equality, an organisation dedicated to securing the right of same-sex couples to marry in Ireland. I met many prominent gay rights activists that day and heard several impassioned pleas from speakers to the effect that the right to marry should not be reserved solely for persons of the opposite sex. Same-sex couples should not be discriminated against in law because of who they love. What's more, advocacy for same-sex marriage, reflecting that gay and lesbian people embraced the ancient institution and dispelling historic stereotypes about their lifestyles, was characterised as a conservative position.

I will never forget looking around the massive room, which was jam-packed with people full of commitment and energy for what was a top priority for them, and realising that I was almost surely the sole attendee who did not concur with what was being said from the podium. To me back then, marriage was the sacred union of one man and one woman to the exclusion of all others. That internalised definition was not for changing. And, after all, civil unions or partnerships offered a similar standing and protections under the law. That would accommodate some of the wholly justified concerns within the LGBT community and preserve the unique standing of traditional marriage. However, that single event, together with other considerations, forced me to rethink a stance that was rooted in my faith and upbringing.

The two principal considerations were my own marriage in 2009 and the 2004 legalisation of same-sex marriage back in Massachusetts following a decision of its Supreme Judicial Court. Getting married to someone I love made me far more receptive to listening to the same-sex couples at the marriage equality gala who were being denied the same right. Their personal stories were heartrending and compelling. My religion discerns a difference between their love and the love between me and my wife. The Catholic Church has the right, which I would defend, to recognise and perform marriages only between persons of the opposite sex. The more I thought about it, though, I could see no valid justification for a government to differentiate and deny its citizens equality of access to civil marriage on this basis.

Also, the alarmist assertions about the legalisation of same-sex marriage in Massachusetts had proved wildly inaccurate. Despite what had been claimed by opponents, there was not a shred of evidence that children suffered or were disadvantaged as a result. Following the controversial court case that precipitated it, same-sex couples got married. It was no big deal. The sky did not fall in. Theirs remained a very small percentage of the overall number of marriages. Marriage equality did not affect existing marriages, nor did it stop tens of thousands of heterosexual couples from taking the plunge. It became settled law and a fact of life, and people moved on.

In 2004, my primary objection to marriage equality becoming law in Massachusetts was how it had come about: through the judicial branch of government. We lawyers have an array of different perspectives on when judicial interpretation crosses the line and becomes judicial lawmaking. Most of us can agree, however, that it is typically better for issues involving deep moral questions to be resolved by the broader citizenry or their representatives, rather than by unelected judges. Altering the nature of the marital relationship is a significant move. When it stems from an interpretation of constitutional provisions by a small handful of jurists who are perceived (often correctly) to be from a privileged background, its legitimacy is far more amenable to attack by opponents as undemocratic. This is particularly the case, as it was with forced busing in Boston, when the alleged negative impact of the decision will not ever be experienced by the judges – the elite, it might be said – responsible for it.

At any rate, following unsuccessful litigation instigated by Katherine Zappone and her long-time partner Ann-Louise Gilligan (who she had married in British Columbia), it was vastly preferable that the voters of Ireland would decide on marriage equality in a referendum to amend the Constitution, notwithstanding the valid concerns of many in the LGBT community about the majority determining what the rights of the minority are. I see their perspective; the possible shortcomings and offence caused are outweighed by the countervailing considerations, in my view, though. A referendum – in which the people would be informed and could then exercise their independent judgement in the privacy of the ballot box and were not constrained by the tremendous political pressure that TDs would have come under – was the best means for advancing constitutional change on same-sex marriage.

At the outset of the campaign, opinion surveys showed that the Yes side had a reasonably solid edge. But the strategists in Yes Equality, the main organisation advocating for marriage equality (there were plenty of affiliated individuals and groupings), did not take anything for granted. They recognised that younger people, who were most instinctively sympathetic, were less likely to be registered to vote or to turn up to cast a ballot on polling day. They also believed that some of the support was soft and that things would tighten as the campaign got underway. Furthermore, they understood that many older people might be uneasy with altering the nature of marriage as they had known it, as might those living in rural Ireland who tended to be more culturally conservative and more likely to be practising Catholics. Following consultation with international advocates, they devised several key tactics to overcome these challenges which came together in a relatively seamless web.

The first was to use the world wide web, and social media platforms in particular, to engage with younger people who increasingly lived, worked and socialised online. The Yes Equality campaign studied what had been successful in campaigns elsewhere; they imitated it to some extent and tailored their communications on Facebook and Twitter for an Irish audience. The digital element of the campaign was immensely impactful and even spawned the #hometovote slogan in which young emigrants around the world told their stories of returning home and casting votes – not in compliance with the law in some instances, it should be said – for marriage equality.

In terms of reaching the centre ground and 'persuadable' voters, the Yes Equality team, while empathising with the entirely legitimate, though politically counterproductive, righteous anger in the LGBT community, knew that they had to make the referendum about the deeply personal stories of those who had been denied the right to marry the person they loved. Their dedicated canvassers both encouraged questions of all sorts and related moving stories. And there was no shortage of men and women who came forward publicly to share how being regarded as somehow lesser in the eyes of the law made them feel.

This latter approach worked exceptionally well and convinced a not insignificant group of sceptics that backing marriage equality was the right thing to do. At a personal level, I had already decided to vote Yes before the campaign and wrote several opinion pieces making the case why observant Catholic voters should do the same because it was the just thing to do and because the referendum was about civil marriage and would not have any bearing on religious marriage. At any rate, the Yes side won handily, 62% to 38%, and the scenes of jubilation in Dublin and around the country on that beautiful day in May of 2015 are etched into Ireland's collective memory. International newspaper headlines conveyed a sense of shock that 'Catholic Ireland' had defied the Church and had embraced social progressivism.

Indeed, the nation had changed. It was palpable to anyone who had visited here in recent years. And as an interview in the *Sunday Business Post* immediately before the historic vote with Colm O'Gorman, the director of Amnesty International Ireland, clearly signalled, campaigners had the 8th Amendment on abortion squarely in their sights. I thought it was a misstep – that he was unwise to speak about this second, far more emotive and divisive issue prior to the first 'big ask' from the people. Not for the first or last time, yet guided by my heart more than my head on this occasion, I was wrong.

The Irish Citizens' Assembly recommended the removal of the 8th Amendment from the Constitution, which provided that: 'The State acknowledges the right to life of the unborn and, with due regard to the equal right to life of the mother, guarantees in its laws to respect, and, as far as practicable, by its laws to defend and vindicate that right.' Their preference was not a shock, given the myriad controversies and widespread anger it had engendered since its adoption in 1983. What was surprising was that the assembly's proposed new legal regime was quite permissive on abortion and that an Oireachtas committee put forward relatively liberal legislation that would come into force in the event that the 8th Amendment was repealed. That legislation would allow for abortion without any restriction as to the reason for the first 12 weeks of a pregnancy. In short, when the campaign began, the electorate knew that, if a majority decided to expunge the 8th Amendment, this would be the new legal regime on abortion.

Unlike on same-sex marriage, my perspective on abortion – stemming partly from my faith and partly from my own moral compass – had not changed. If anything, the personal experience of watching Eileen give birth to our son only reinforced my view that every human life – from the innocent, vulnerable unborn child all the way to the monstrous individual who has been convicted of the most heinous of crimes and is on death row in the US – is sacred and worth standing up for. I am neither a radical nor an evangelist; I completely get why family members, friends and colleagues strongly disagree. Yet I also am aware that my heartfelt conviction against abortion has made people look askance at or draw harsh conclusions about me, that it would have been a serious impediment to my running for office in the Democratic Party in Massachusetts, that it has cost me friends and created enemies, and that it has made many things a lot harder and more awkward than they ever should have been. I think that's all terribly unfair, but so be it.

That said, I was never a fan of the 8th Amendment. I do not believe that abortion belongs in a nation's cornerstone document, especially because 'constitutionalising' the issue inevitably brings it into the judicial realm, when it is an inescapably political matter. Whether it is seen as a question of life or death, as anti-abortionists claim, or of a woman's bodily autonomy, as pro-choicers assert, the laws around it should be made democratically by the people and their elected representatives, not by generally unaccountable judges.

I had this much in common with the many practitioners and legal academics who had long championed the removal of the 8th Amendment and then united as Lawyers for Yes. It was strange, then, that my fellow lawyers would simultaneously defend the *Roe v Wade* US Supreme Court precedent from 1973. In that seminal case, the country's highest court ruled that its precedent, which had created a constitutional right to privacy that rendered laws banning contraception null and void, extended to allow women in America the right to terminate a pregnancy with certain restrictions.

Interestingly, it was this line of US jurisprudence that led to anti-abortion activists advocating furiously for constitutional protection for the unborn child because the Irish Supreme Court, in *McGee v Attorney General* (also in 1973), struck down a law effectively prohibiting the use of contraceptives by married couples and referred to the similar US case, *Griswold v Connecticut* (1965), in doing so. Terrified that their own Supreme Court would take a similar next step, the Pro-Life Amendment Campaign was founded in 1981 and the 8th Amendment was enshrined in the Constitution by an overwhelming popular vote in 1983.

Just as removing the 8th Amendment would transfer abortion into the political sphere, the overturning of *Roe* would not make abortion illegal in America. It would send a highly charged question back to local legislators to decide what the law should be in their respective jurisdictions. This is precisely what Together for Yes was seeking. To me, it was an 'ends justify the means' inconsistency. Regardless, I would have joined them in voting in favour of the repeal of the 8th Amendment if it were not for the legislation in the offing that would swiftly take its place. Twelve weeks of unrestricted access to abortion was something my conscience could not countenance.

The polls unanimously suggested a Yes outcome from the beginning. Unfortunately for abortion opponents, the result was never really in doubt. The No side did the best it could, yet was overwhelmed in the end by an outstanding, passion-fuelled campaign from the Together for Yes group who raised a tremendous sum of money and energised a broad coalition comprising older, seasoned activists who remembered the 'bad old days' of 1983 and young people who deemed the 8th Amendment an artefact from an awful past they couldn't quite imagine. In particular, women of all ages banded together in this cause. Some of us thought that the Yes side was sluggish at first and that the vote had to be closer than the previous referendum on same-sex marriage was. A landslide 66%–34% triumph put paid to these notions. I, for one, was stunned that the margin of victory was even higher than it had been three years previously. And again, Ireland's decisive statement generated headlines around the globe. The *New York Times*, for example, reported that 'Ireland votes to legalise abortion in blow to Catholic conservatism'.

There is no doubt but that the pace of social change in Ireland went from 0 to 100 in a very short space of time. The two votes proved just how off the mark politicians, who are presumed to be very attuned to the thinking of the people in whose design their electoral fate rests, can sometimes be. Since then, more than a few who were reticent have insinuated that they were right there with the agitators for some time. This is manifestly untrue. With a few exceptions, Irish politicians were resolutely reluctant to go anywhere near same-sex marriage and even more afraid of abortion. It turns out that society was way ahead of them, and well ahead of many political pundits, too. Their verdicts in 2015 and 2018 were crystal clear.

Nonetheless, two connected aspects of these two democratic revolutions heralding a new dawn in a transformed nation still trouble me. And the vote tallies showed that the transformation truly was national. Unlike in the US, where Alabama would have voted decisively against both referendums and California would have done the opposite, just one Irish constituency in each voted No, and by the slimmest of margins. Conservative attitudes persisted in rural areas, yet the societal change was arguably more pronounced in them than in urban areas. Conversely, if anything, 'red state America' has gone even further to the right. Against this backdrop, I speak as one of what I suspect is a small cohort of people whose votes were split in the referendums. And I fully respect and understand the viewpoints and rationale of those who took the opposite stance to me on same-sex marriage and abortion.

My first concern is that some of the victors do not have any warmth of feeling or empathy for those they vanquished. In particular, the repeal of the 8th Amendment was portrayed as something of an emancipation of Irish women from a patriarchal order and a state that was dominated by an inherently misogynistic Roman Catholic Church. The documentary on the Together for Yes campaign is tellingly entitled 'When Women Won'. I can see why. But where does that leave the approximately 30% of Irish women who voted No for a whole host of reasons? Many in this minority surely felt unable to share their thoughts and feelings with female family and friends for fear of being judged negatively; others who courageously did consequently found themselves either gently or explicitly ostracised in all likelihood.

Moreover, the common implication that those who did not back marriage equality are inherently homophobic is wide of the mark. To be sure, some No voters regrettably were motivated by homophobia. But others simply could not be dissuaded from a sincere belief in how marriage has been defined and known for centuries. One can disagree with them without questioning their motives or character. On the flip side, the eagerness with which some social conservatives have assumed a victimhood status and asserted far-reaching bias against them is overwrought and just plain untrue. Much of this posturing reveals a convenient, wilful ignorance of the fashion in which women, in particular, who either dared to disagree or who fell afoul of its teachings were treated by the Catholic Church in Ireland, allegedly in the name of a loving God, for far too long. By way of compelling example, the publication of the Report on Mother and Baby Homes was a chronicle of evil perpetrated by the Church and aided and abetted by the organs of the state, and by society more broadly.

My second worry relates to the place of the Church in a republic that has so enthusiastically endorsed secularism. Where next for the institution and for its faithful followers when a clear majority of the citizenry has effectively repudiated core teachings and has either left the religion altogether or barely practises it? Of course, it is for the best that the Church has nowhere approaching the total power it formerly exercised and abused so malevolently in mother and baby homes and myriad other settings. Divesting schools of Catholic patronage appropriately continues, albeit at too slow a pace for some campaigners. I do wonder, however, about what may be lost in this purge. My faith – and I should say that this extends to those of other religious traditions – is a source of incredible strength in my life. I lean upon it during trying periods. There are lots who feel the exact same.

Additionally, I think it's vital to stay mindful that, wherever there are people in this world who are struggling, vulnerable and marginalised, the Church is there for them. Whether it's Sister Stan promoting the rights of immigrants in a country with a tendency to forget that it used to be a nation of emigrants or Brother Kevin feeding the homeless at the Capuchin Day Centre in Dublin or missionaries who work with and minister to the poorest of the poor in Africa, the Church does amazing things for those most in need every day, everywhere. Those in Ireland who dwell on the grievous wrongs it has undeniably done should remember both the extraordinary good that it does in its outreach and the positive influence it has on the lives of the faithful.

I suspect that being more cognisant of its good work, and not just of its bad deeds, might make some who have drifted away reconsider their relationship with the Church they were brought up in. At the same time, the Church's leadership – from the Vatican to diocesan priests – should emphasise what being an active Catholic can do for the flock, not what the flock can and cannot do because they are Catholic. In truth, and speaking from experience, one's realisation of the former typically leads to one's fulfilment of the latter.

This is something I am trying to foster in Larry Óg, who is growing up in a country that is vastly different from the one that existed a mere generation ago where Catholicism was foisted on the young people. That's not the way it is any more. Rightly so. And just as young people in the US have reinvigorated the progressive wing of the Democratic Party, their counterparts in Ireland are shaping this country's future in so many different areas. Above all, that is true in politics and governance – domestically, as well as at European and international levels. The dramatic social change that flowed from their active participation in the same-sex marriage and abortion referendums demonstrates their growing potency. How might their impact be felt in Irish politics in the decades to come?

CHAPTER 17

The Future of Irish Politics

It may have been overwhelmed shortly afterward by the onset of COVID-19, but Ireland's general election in February of 2020 was a watershed moment in the country's political history. Sinn Féin, long consigned to outlier status owing largely to its having been identified as the political wing of the IRA, had an extraordinary result. The outcome was a virtual three-way draw with the two big centrist beasts of Irish politics, Fianna Fáil and Fine Gael. Having performed horribly in local and European elections in 2019, almost no one saw their unprecedentedly strong showing coming.

Even the party itself did not see it. If they had, they surely would have recruited and run more candidates. For Sinn Féin topped the ballot in many constituencies and a second candidate likely could have taken a seat in several of these. Additionally, the successful runners included some who were relatively unknown and untested. It was fantastic for the party and it could have been even better. The outcome forced Fianna Fáil and Fine Gael into what had previously been unthinkable: a coalition government comprised of them and the Green Party, with the position of Taoiseach to rotate between the larger two. The nature of this arrangement, and how Sinn Féin and other mainly leftist parties and groupings would collaborate in opposition, was the subject of much speculation among political watchers.

But then a pandemic arrived on this island. And politics as we have always known it, broadly speaking, was in suspended animation for the next 15 months or so. When coronavirus became a clear and present danger in March 2020, Leo Varadkar, in the US where he was on the annual St. Patrick's Day visit to the White House, delivered a memorable address about the fight that lay ahead for the country. Varadkar isn't thought of as an inspiring orator, yet it was a superb speech which both laid out the gravity of the situation facing the people and the nation and sounded a note of optimism that we could collectively rise to this unfortunate occasion. Having fared poorly in the general election just a month beforehand, it helped Fine Gael's standing in the polls. And in opinion surveys conducted since, Fine Gael and Sinn Féin have been fighting it out for the top spot, with the lead party in government, Fianna Fáil, some distance behind. How the government is perceived to have managed a frightening public health crisis, as well as the economic and other ramifications of COVID-19, will be big issues in the next general election. And housing is the biggest of them all.

It remains to be seen, though, how much can be extrapolated from what has transpired in this unprecedented period about the years that will follow it. Now that some semblance of normality has been restored, the issues that have dominated as of late – housing (first and foremost), health, Brexit fallout, education, socio-economic rights, the rural vs urban divide, etc. – will again return to the fore. In this vein, it is worth examining the challenges and opportunities for the individual political parties and pondering some of the overarching questions about the future of Irish politics that either have presented themselves already, or soon will.

Ahead of the 2020 general election, it was widely felt that Fianna Fáil would come out on top and that its leader, Micheál Martin, would thereby avoid becoming the party's sole leader not to serve as Taoiseach. The assessment of Harry McGee, political correspondent with the *Irish Times*, was broadly shared. McGee posited that Fianna Fáil would win 53 seats in the 160-member Dáil, with 33 and 28 going to Fine Gael and Sinn Féin, respectively. That Martin's party won just 38, a loss of seven seats, meant that internal strife was rampant from the moment the votes were tallied, even though they did elect the most TDs by a whisker. Ever since, Martin's tenure as Taoiseach in a turbulent time has been routinely overshadowed by rumblings of discontent with his leadership and by rumours about potential heaves against him.

In fairness to the Cork man, however, his task was not an easy one. In short, the long dominant entity in Irish politics is in the throes of existential tumult. What is Fianna Fáil in 2021? Martin has endeavoured to make it more progressive, partly because that's where his heart is and also with an eye to improving its currently poor standing in Dublin and among young people. The consequences of his mission to better the party's fortunes have been decidedly mixed. Left-of-centre voters don't buy the repackaging. Advocating for 'moving with the times' and a concomitant, albeit subtle, nod to its critics that the party of Éamon de Valera is out of step has only embittered a lot of his colleagues in the parliamentary party. And some of the party's formerly dependable grassroots supporters have gravitated to Sinn Féin, independents (some of whom are originally Fianna Fáilers) or even to the fledgling Aontú. And now, every potential pivot in messaging and emphasis carries as much risk as it does potential reward. There is no easy answer for Fianna Fáil – no matter who the party is led by.

From my own perspective, Fianna Fáil had been the party our family was instinctively sympathetic to. My uncle was close to its leadership and my father always said that its politicians were the nearest thing to Boston Irish Democrats like us. Dad thoroughly abhorred Sinn Féin because of its association with the IRA and often said that 'its Marxist economics would destroy Ireland', while muttering to himself about 'clueless Irish-Americans' who had no idea of their policies other than reunification. In truth, the average Irish-American knows next to nothing about politics in the Republic and has a superficial understanding of the North. This is not to condemn them; there is little reason for busy people in Chicago or New York to be actively engaged in matters that don't ordinarily affect their day-to-day lives. But it does mean that some should be more cautious about holding themselves out as experts and voicing strong opinions in an authoritative tone when their knowledge doesn't scratch the surface. The Donnellys took it far more seriously and, just as we gravitated to the moderate nationalism of John Hume and the SDLP in the North, we were drawn to Fianna Fáil in the Republic. While I have given first preference votes to other parties and independents in the past, I am predisposed to Fianna Fáil.

The party's long-time competitor for supremacy in the crucial centre ground, Fine Gael, finds itself in a much better place in 2021. While there are those who just can't figure out why and some of the shine has definitely come off the persona, Leo Varadkar remains a very popular leader who, as a gay man with an Indian father, enjoys a global reputation as the face of modern Ireland. Moreover, Fine Gael boasts a cadre of young, energetic, articulate and able politicians who are also extremely strong media performers, such as Simon Coveney, Helen McEntee, Paschal Donohoe, Simon Harris and Jennifer Carroll MacNeill. They have excelled in their various briefs and uniformly project an aura of competence. They quite clearly enjoy the broad support of Ireland's middle-class voters and their blend of right-of-centre economics with cultural progressivism is in many ways a mirror image of the prevalent zeitgeist at present. Without asserting that Fianna Fáil is lacking in talent – there is plenty – these Fine Gael politicians have played a significant role, both before and during the pandemic, in dealing a major blow to the former's support among professional people and business owners.

Sinn Féin has a similarly solid roster of excellent, persuasive and appealing individuals who are well known to the public. Mary Lou McDonald succeeded Gerry Adams, an obviously immense historical figure around the globe who is synonymous both with the IRA's violent past and the transition of the republican movement into mainstream politics. To her great credit, the south Dublin native took his place and made it her own in every imaginable way. At least in public, there has never been as much as a whisper to the effect that 'Adams would have done x, y or z better than Mary Lou.' Even allowing for the reality that Sinn Féin is not a traditional political party – its enemies would contend that it is still run as if it were a paramilitary organisation – this is a feat in and of itself. Like her or loathe her, McDonald is a powerhouse of a politician. Her colleagues Pearse Doherty, Louise O'Reilly and Eoin Ó Broin are top-notch communicators and advocates.

In the short interlude between the 2020 general election and COVID, there was plenty of speculation as to where the Sinn Féin vote came from. There had long been a ceiling on their support which correlated fairly closely with the electorate's collective memory of the IRA's numerous acts of malfeasance during the Troubles. How had this been smashed? To be sure, Sinn Féin captured the support of many young people who cannot afford their own homes and fear that they will struggle more financially than their parents did, despite being well-educated and holding down good jobs. And their firmly leftist disposition on an array of issues garnered them the backing of others beyond their stridently nationalist, working-class base. To these younger and increasingly desperate voters, Sinn Féin's past really is ancient history. They would point to the not-entirely-peaceful incarnations of the other parties with some justification. And they are not so moved about what might have occurred in the context of a complex conflict. Rather, they want to know how on earth they will manage to obtain what is missing from their lives: home ownership and genuine, lasting economic security.

But there was more to it than this. Indeed, casting a ballot for Sinn Féin arguably became an outlet for the anger of a wider cross-section of the Irish people who are dispirited at the direction of the country and frustrated by what they view to be the establishment's exercise of control over Ireland. While Mary Lou McDonald and her team admirably have never either expressly or implicitly courted men and women who see immigration or the European Union in a wholly negative light, some of that ilk undeniably saw placing a tick next to the Sinn Féin candidate on the ballot paper as the best means of venting their displeasure. Indeed, surveys have shown that the party's voters are more likely than others to favour the system of Direct Provision for refugees and asylum seekers and tighter controls on immigration. And on social media platforms frequented by members of Sinn Féin, the use of sexist and racist terms and additional offensive language has been shown to be fairly common.

For three of the other parties on the left, the Greens, Labour and the Social Democrats, it is this suspicion about what Sinn Féin actually is, together with a revulsion at its past, that renders doing business with them in the form of a left-wing coalition a still-remote happening for now. The far-left groupings mightn't necessarily share the same discomfort about events of previous decades, yet would vigorously dispute that Sinn Féin is a principled socialist party and seems determined to resist joining forces on that basis.

Naturally, that the left appears destined to be factionalised for the short to medium term is good news for Fine Gael and Fianna Fáil. As recently as 2007, the two moderate parties won more than two-thirds of the vote. That had fallen to 43% by 2020. It is true to say that, relatively speaking, the centre has held in Irish politics, but to nowhere approaching the same extent that it once did. As hampered as Sinn Féin may currently be insofar as it is deemed untouchable by all of its counterparts – watch that space, though! – the path back to anything close to the endorsement of a majority of the people for either Fine Gael or Fianna Fáil is narrow and full of obstacles.

In sum, the future of Irish politics is murky, full of known unknowns. It has been posited that things are leading inexorably toward realignment – or what may be more accurately labelled a recalibration – along roughly left and right lines with Sinn Féin and Fine Gael as the central protagonists, tilting as needs be in order to receive the support of other parties and independents necessary to form sustainable governments. The combative language employed by the representatives of each in the Dáil and on broadcast and social media suggests that they are spoiling for this mano-a-mano clash.

In this scenario, the two parties would march, or muddle, on without any dramatic changes in focus or personnel and enjoy somewhere between one-quarter and one-third of the voters staying faithfully in their corner. This analysis further presumes that there is no realistic way back for Fianna Fáil – that, on the one hand, it will not successfully retain its deeply nationalist, populist, Catholic identity and simultaneously attract a different, more diverse following and that, on the other, no alternative strategy to achieve broader buy-in can be drawn up and activated by a party that has always been so adept at adapting.

While something approximating this eventuality is eminently plausible, it is going a good deal too far to presume that it is likely. They have an enviable wealth of stellar performers right now, yet Fine Gael has never done politics as well as Fianna Fáil. That they are so esteemed by the middle class – both stylistically and substantively – could ultimately prove their undoing in a country where snobbery is a mortal sin and those perceived to have notions above their station are immediately targeted to be taken down a notch or two. Their response to what has been wrought by COVID-19 and housing proposals will be interesting in this respect.

Moreover, if Sinn Féin's base continues to develop as an unwieldy entity of idealistic leftists, committed republicans, disenchanted young people and angry voters who might otherwise gravitate toward a party of the hard right, those tensions will inevitably rise to the surface and could precipitate division. It is also crucial to remember that it's easy to attack from the outside. Governing ain't easy.

This will come to the fore in the context of addressing the toughest conundrum of all in Irish politics in 2021: the seemingly intractable shortage of reasonably priced housing. Housing is *the* defining issue at present. Since the low point in the early part of the last decade, the cost of homes in Dublin and across the country has grown exponentially. There are many people, ranging in age up to their 50s, who cannot purchase a place to call their own. This includes well-educated, relatively high-earning couples with young children, as well as single people in an even more difficult position. There is a definite thirst for government intervention on a grand scale to make home ownership a reality for thousands currently in limbo. Fine Gael and Fianna Fáil are widely perceived to have been too reliant historically on the private sector and too cosy with developers. Voters regard Sinn Féin as better placed to tackle the crisis.

A key question, then, is whether some older people, who may be affluent and have had a deep enmity for Sinn Féin, could find it in themselves give the erstwhile provisional wing of the IRA a high preference in a general election because they are so aggrieved by the very unsatisfactory situation facing their children, grandchildren and the rest of their contemporaries? When Sinn Féin does enter government, it will have no room to hide or prevaricate; the party will have to make some hard choices and then endure the wrath of those who are adversely affected. That's what being in government entails. It will be fascinating to gauge the reaction of the diverse cohort of voters who will have gotten them to the 'promised land' after they are let down in some respects, which they will be.

Uncertainty abounds in this milieu. And I don't have a crystal ball. Returning to the here and now, the Irish people can take pride in the fact that, with few exceptions, the country's politicians have behaved like adults and acted responsibly in response to coronavirus. Additionally, notwithstanding some vitriolic exchanges on social media, political discourse here is relatively civil and hasn't descended to the depths it has in Ireland's neighbours across the Atlantic Ocean or the Irish Sea. Government ministers are near universally respected because of how well informed they are and how they comport themselves in the most important forums. It's been said before and bears repeating: Ireland punches way above its weight internationally. The country's politicians and diplomats deserve a great deal of praise for what has been accomplished as a result.

The doors of Joe Biden's White House are wide open to Ireland. This presents tremendous further opportunities. But the world should not labour under any illusions: President Biden's focus is on taking the required steps to heal a wounded America. It has to be. This job is a daunting one and there is much damage to repair. That the US is in a bad state was clear for anyone to see during the Trump presidency. The problems, however, predate the improbable rise of the bombastic New York billionaire.

CHAPTER 18

The Origins of Political 'Polarisation'

A s my uncle recalls with something approaching nostalgia, those on the ideological poles in both parties were in the minority when he was serving in the House of Representatives from the late 1970s to early 1990s. Moderates – or put another way, sensible people – still held sway and routinely exercised a necessary brake on the fanatical impulses of those so blinded by conviction that they had lost sight of reality. From 1983 to 1985, in bi-partisan votes, a divided 98th Congress made Martin Luther King's birthday a federal holiday, helped to preserve the solvency of social security, revised the federal criminal law and approved deficit reduction measures. In the 1980s, my uncle worked with Republicans in the House and Ted Kennedy helped him by enlisting GOP colleagues in the Senate to pass the Donnelly Visa legislation.

There were conservative Democrats and liberal Republicans; individual members of Congress weren't as amenable to rigid classification and were less likely to follow the party whip on a host of issues where they deviated from dogma. Deals were regularly cut, and often stemmed from strong personal relationships. Members of the House and the Senate might have contrasting perspectives and have represented parts of the country whose interests almost inherently conflicted, yet they broadly shared a sense that they were working for the common good of the American people.

Where did it all go so badly wrong? It is a complicated question that is not amenable to a straightforward answer. Additionally, opinion formers in the pundit class and academia have framed the division in a way that suits a particular world view, but does not necessarily reflect the nuance of what has happened, nor does it paint a completely accurate picture of where American politics, writ large, now is. In assessing and accounting for such rapid transformation, the role of the inextricably intertwined forces of globalisation and technology must be examined, as well as the parts played by the exalted status of money in American politics, a tax code literally drafted by the wealthy for the wealthy, a grossly politicised process for drawing up congressional districts and a media ecosystem that has contributed to politics being regarded as merely another type of entertainment.

It may be trite to say, but a mere half century ago, computers and information technology were in their infancy. Communication, other than by telephone or telegraph, was slow. Heavy industry, mines, mills and factories were still abundant across the US, especially in its interior, and many young men and women graduated from high school, did not seek a third-level qualification yet could still count on long-term, well-paid employment in them. The idea of 24-hour cable news networks was just that, an idea. And platforms such as Twitter and Facebook were unimaginable. The sweeping changes since have transformed all aspects of our lives – both for good and for ill.

There was a technological boom and a lot of people became multimillionaires virtually overnight. They were often quite young and tended to be clustered on the coasts, near to the prestigious colleges and universities where they had been educated and where the innovations of their dreams were developed, adjusted and nurtured into being. The internet and email were their progeny. Simultaneously, blue-collar jobs were steadily being exported to Mexico and elsewhere in the developing world where labour costs were far lower and environmental regulations were less burdensome. Non-stop news, online and on cable TV, slowly displaced daily newspapers and scheduled news bulletins. Social media pioneers became instant billionaires and the influence of their brands surpassed even their wildest expectations. And in terms of coarsening public discourse and exacerbating societal divisions, that influence has been pernicious.

Nothing in this perfunctory recitation of seminal events since the early 1970s is novel or revelatory. But it somehow doesn't feature as prominently as it should when pundits discuss the lamentable political atmosphere that has grown up at the same time. The big tech and related money soon found its way into the political sphere on the west coast, where successful entrepreneurs and those they employed in well-remunerated positions dabbled in politics, usually from a leftist perspective, and the costs of living and campaigning increased dramatically. Their priorities and the things that mattered most to them diverged significantly from the 'bread and butter' issues that the Democratic Party had always stood on. Money talks, however. The east coast followed, though it took longer, primarily owing to the strength of labour unions and a cadre of urban, ethnic Catholic Democrats who resisted the new direction urged by well-heeled benefactors.

Meanwhile, many of these suddenly unemployed or underemployed blue-collar workers discovered that, at a national level, the party to which they had long been wedded did not represent them as zealously as it once had. Other special interests, which they were quite hostile to in some instances, had taken precedence. The clash was most obvious with respect to the Democrats' embrace of a secular agenda on cultural issues. It also was manifest on racial justice and environmental concerns. Those who dissented and felt betrayed by the party found a vehicle for their anger in a former Hollywood actor, Ronald Reagan, who played to an audience he knew he could win over. Reagan Democrats – whose collective slogan was 'we didn't leave our party; our party left us' – were a decisive voting bloc in the 1980s and helped Reagan crush the incumbent Jimmy Carter in 1980 and absolutely destroy Walter Mondale in 1984.

These Americans didn't rally around President Reagan solely on economic or cultural issues. He appealed to their patriotism at a juncture when communism and the Soviet Union were still deemed to be threats. Both met their end during his tenure. That 'good vs evil' prism through which people in the US then saw the rest of the world was a great unifier. Even though income inequality was on the rise, the 1980s was a good economic period for most. Additionally, Reagan spoke the language of conservatives and disaffected Democrats on the so-called culture wars. He was popular enough that his vice-president, George HW Bush, was selected to continue where he had left off. A genuine war hero of strong moral character, Bush was nonetheless a weak standard-bearer who couldn't connect with people the same way as his ex-boss did, yet managed to win the presidency because the Democratic nominee, Michael Dukakis, was quite easy to caricature as a dispassionate, Massachusetts liberal.

On the election of George Bush Sr, the equation was reasonably straightforward. Democrats, at least in the context of presidential elections, had drifted too far away from the centre, where these contests are won or lost. The parties were more clearly defined as right and left in a way they hadn't been previously. That state of play was severely complicated shortly thereafter. First, there was the war in Iraq which the US may have won, yet which marked the commencement of decades of Middle East interventionism that had devastating consequences for the participants and for so many innocent men, women and children. Second, Bill Clinton, a centrist Democrat and an infinitely superior politician to the man he vanquished, came into power and wholeheartedly endorsed NAFTA, which further accelerated the export of blue-collar jobs. The fallout from these events blurred the right vs left partisan divide.

The 1992 presidential election should be remembered for what it foreshadowed above all else. The brilliant writer and gifted communicator (whether you like him or loathe him), Pat Buchanan, furious at President Bush for embarking upon an unnecessary and unwinnable course of action in the Middle East, took on the incumbent and almost beat him in the New Hampshire primary. A Texas billionaire and independent, Ross Perot, sounded the bell against internationalism and purported free trade and took 19% of the vote in the general election. Bill Clinton had Perot to thank for his triumph. Buoyed by big donors and his own popularity, Clinton enjoyed high approval ratings and a successful presidency that was besmirched only by a tawdry sex scandal and a wholly unnecessary impeachment.

Buchanan and Perot may go down as footnotes in history, but they grasped what was happening and were ahead of the curve in their messaging. Why were working-class and poor young Americans being sent thousands of miles away to be cannon fodder when there was no direct threat posed to America's vital interests? Why did the Democratic Party's highest elected officials enthusiastically back trade deals that would inevitably take away the livelihoods and, hence, ruin the lives of countless men and women? The anger of millions seethed and occasionally surfaced, notwithstanding the concerted efforts of establishment-oriented Republicans and Democrats to sweep it away.

The second Bush barely snuck into the White House at a moment when the country was disgusted by the X-rated details of his predecessor's private life that were broadcast for all to hear. A temporary moment of global solidarity after 9/11 was quickly eroded by a wholly indefensible military response in Iraq and Afghanistan. Many Americans were killed in these conflicts; even more came back with physical and mental wounds that will never heal. Their fellow citizens were appalled and, when a charismatic and visionary African-American who called upon people to have hope, Barack Obama, came on the scene, they took the plunge. His presidency delivered expanded access to healthcare, an enormous feat in and of itself, and not much else. Through no big fault of his own, income inequality heightened, as did political division. There was a racial backlash against President Obama, too, perhaps most evident in elements of the Tea Party movement.

The Tea Party's founding leadership was primarily dedicated to a radical implementation of fiscally conservative principles and to small government, and placed little emphasis on cultural issues. It was a strong force within the Republican Party for a time. Many activists were eventually drawn to it as they saw it as an umbrella under which to fit other right-wing beliefs. Its composition grew more heterogeneous and the Tea Party actually morphed into an entity that was quite at odds with the intentions of its luminaries and with how it was portrayed in the media.

The changing character of the Tea Party movement was consistent with what was lurking just under the surface in America. The upper echelons of the two parties determinedly refused to acknowledge it, in large part because it was anathema to the wealthy donors whose bidding they did as a matter of course. Their interests were not nuanced and lay in buying the loyalty of politicians of all stripes. Some of what they lobbied for related to causes near and dear to true believers on the left and on the right. Their money helped to kill off moderates as a species on Capitol Hill and in statehouses. Also, the process of drawing congressional districts is inherently political and corruptible. Powerful special interests played their part in ensuring that the vast majority of these districts are now reliably Democratic or Republican. The two parties, particularly the GOP, colluded in this mutually beneficial arrangement.

The overarching goal of the most powerful special interests boiled down to one thing, and it's not overly glib to put it this bluntly: make the already rich even richer. The tax code was doctored and tinkered with accordingly. Supposed reforms collectively favoured the haves at the expense of the have-nots. The gulf between them expanded exponentially. To their shame, Democrats put raising money and the corporatist agenda that accompanied those dollars ahead of the needs of the ordinary Americans. And Republicans had always favoured the wealthy, yet had managed to use 'hot button' cultural issues to win over people who the party platform paid mere lip service to on everything else.

What lay and grew beneath, however, were exactly the sentiments that Ross Perot and Pat Buchanan had expressed in the early 1990s. In pure political terms, the eccentric Texas billionaire and the deeply conservative, orthodox Catholic were flawed prophets. But they presciently identified where a substantial segment of the American people stood. Opinion surveys reflected it increasingly as the years went by.

These men and women were tired of pointless wars which had disproportionately cost or wrecked the lives of their family members and friends. They did not think America should police the world or involve itself anywhere, unless the country's narrowly defined vital interests were imperilled. The nation's leaders should worry about the struggles of Americans first. They were sceptical of international institutions that they believe the US pays for and derives next to nothing from. They rejected the notion that an open, free market economy and consequent trade agreements inevitably benefit all, having seen so many left behind and destitute in their wake.

They saw the exorbitant cost of higher education as an impediment to their sons and daughters enjoying a better life than they had – a core component of the American Dream. They had deep reservations about the darkening skin tone of the average American and many harboured racist or xenophobic views. They were firmly on one side in the culture wars and abhorred the departure from what they held up as traditional values. They yearned for a simpler time and a country they could actually understand and be proud of again. And they were frustrated with both parties and with politicians who hadn't paid much attention to what they were saying or the extent to which they were hurting.

Their outlook, despite how the media might attempt to simplify it for all sorts of reasons, is not easily amenable to classify as being of the right or the left, at least not in how these labels have historically been conceived of. There are conservative tenets within it, but there are aspects that are downright antithetical to right-wing dogma. Ronald Reagan's dwindling band of disciples, for example, are appalled by what they see as dogmatically leftist opposition to free trade agreements and to an interventionist foreign policy. This can more aptly be described as a third way in a country of more than 300 million people where there are only two major political parties. It is safe to assume that most of them have gravitated toward the Republican Party, yet equally, a sizable chunk voted for Barack Obama and his message of hope in 2008 and 2012.

The media doesn't like complexity and, instead, the discourse focuses on a grossly oversimplified, less-than-accurate depiction of a state of play that pits an uncompromising left against an intolerant right. In fact, the country is splintered along multiple fault lines. It's not black and white. It takes the form of polarisation only because there are just two choices on a ballot paper. In a climate where news and entertainment commonly overlap, where ratings and the corollary bottom line in terms of advertising revenue are the dominant animating impulse, this is only logical. Try to keep it simple and the dollars will keep coming in.

Yet this does a tremendous disservice to journalism and to the American polity more broadly. Moreover, it perpetuates misconceptions about what the true state of play is and arguably makes things more toxic than they should be. Regrettably, the eternal chase for the almighty dollar, inextricably intertwined with the huge changes that have taken hold, is largely to blame for the complicated place where the land of my birth has been stuck as of late.

CHAPTER 19

American Malaise

One of the central tenets of the American civic religion is that our nation is a 'city on a hill' – a shining example and beacon of hope to the rest of the world. Although commentators outside the US have quite rightly protested against this sort of exceptionalism and cited a plethora of reasons why this notion, accepted without thinking from within, does not comport with reality, it was regularly repeated by political leaders of both parties.

It was a particular favourite of Ronald Reagan. In a speech to supporters just before he won the presidency in 1980, he said,

> I have quoted John Winthrop's words more than once on the campaign trail this year – for I believe that Americans in 1980 are every bit as committed to that vision of a shining 'city on a hill', as were those long ago settlers ... These visitors to that city on the Potomac do not come as white or black, red or yellow; they are not Jews or Christians; conservatives or liberals; or Democrats or Republicans. They are Americans awed by what has gone before, proud of what for them is still ... a shining city on a hill.

And when he was leaving office after two terms, he returned to the same theme:

> I've spoken of the shining city all my political life, but I don't know if I ever quite communicated what I saw when I said it. But in my mind it was a tall, proud city built on rocks stronger than oceans, wind-swept, God-blessed, and teeming with people of all kinds living in harmony and peace; a city with free ports that hummed with commerce and creativity. And if there had to be city walls, the walls had doors and the doors were open to anyone with the will and the heart to get here. That's how I saw it, and see it still.

In 2006, a first-term US Senator from Illinois, Barack Obama, adapted this narrative in a commencement address to graduates at the Boston campus of the University of Massachusetts, next door to my alma mater, Boston College High School:

> It was right here, in the waters around us, where the American experiment began. As the earliest settlers arrived on the shores of Boston and Salem and Plymouth, they dreamed of building a City upon a Hill. And the world watched, waiting to see if this improbable idea called America would succeed. More than half of you represent the very first member of your family to ever attend college. In the most diverse university in all of New England, I look out at a sea of faces that are African-American and Hispanic-American and Asian-American and Arab-American. I see students that have come here from over 100 different countries,

believing like those first settlers that they too could find a home in this City on a Hill – that they too could find success in this unlikeliest of places.

Compare their inspired, lofty words with the language employed by President Donald Trump at his inauguration where he assailed 'American carnage' and pledged to put a stop to it.

For many decades, we've enriched foreign industry at the expense of American industry; subsidized the armies of other countries while allowing for the very sad depletion of our military; we've defended other nations' borders while refusing to defend our own; and spent trillions of dollars overseas while America's infrastructure has fallen into disrepair and decay. We've made other countries rich while the wealth, strength, and confidence of our country have disappeared over the horizon. One by one, the factories shuttered and left our shores, with not even a thought about the millions upon millions of American workers left behind. The wealth of our middle class has been ripped from their homes and then redistributed across the entire world. But that is the past. And now we are looking only to the future. We assembled here today are issuing a new decree to be heard in every city, in every foreign capital, and in every hall of power. From this day forward, a new vision will govern our land. From this moment on, it's going to be America First.

Both on traditional and social media in Ireland, the widespread reaction to Trump's first moments in office was one of disgust and outrage. What the new commander-in-chief was describing did not remotely resemble the America that so many Irish people knew and loved. They were right, in the sense that he was talking to geographic parts of and citizens of an America that most foreign visitors have never encountered. Truth be told, they aren't all that familiar to me either. But I recall vividly thinking as I listened to it that, while the speech might not live up to traditional expectations for an inaugural address, he had captured the ascendant mood of fear and negativity about the future in the country. For one opinion survey after another in recent years has revealed that the sense of can-do optimism that had been so integral to the collective character of the US, though not extinguished, no longer burned as brightly in the wake of transformative changes.

Comprehensive polling undertaken by Pew Research Center in 2019 engendered some startling data.[14] A narrow majority, 56%, said they were somewhat or more optimistic about the country's future. In previous decades, surveys reflected omnipresent positivity as to what lay ahead. And answers to detailed questions suggest an even more downbeat outlook. Solid majorities agreed that the national debt will become crippling; that the gulf between rich and poor will widen further; that many workers will be displaced by automation and robotics; that the economy will weaken; that quality healthcare will get more expensive and harder to access; that the environment will deteriorate and that older Americans will

14 Pew Research Center, 'Looking to the Future, Public Sees an America in Decline on Many Fronts' (21 March 2019) available at https://www.pewresearch.org/social-trends/2019/03/21/public-sees-an-america-in-decline-on-many-fronts/ <last accessed 12 May 2021>.

increasingly face poverty; and that a terrorist attack of the magnitude of 9/11 will occur again by 2050. Lastly, some 70% of those asked thought that the country was going in the wrong direction. This was not an abrupt departure in thinking or a result of the Trump presidency. Rather, it was a continuation of a trend.

It is really no surprise in the wake of the aforementioned far-reaching changes brought on by the twin forces of technology and globalisation. The alterations have made multiple elements of modern life much easier, yet their detrimental impacts are demonstrable. The 'giant sucking sound' of manufacturing jobs to Mexico and the developing world forecast by Ross Perot as he pursued the presidency in 1992 did come to pass. Blue-collar workers across the heartland, in their droves, lost well-paid jobs with good benefits, like health insurance for themselves and their families and generous pensions. Where could these newly unemployed men and women turn, especially those of advancing age who had never worked anyplace else and had limited skill sets? For many, the service and retail sectors were the sole options. They could typically expect to be the recipients of a pay cut of a minimum of 50%, to have no health insurance and to face into their later years bereft of a cushion or savings and wholly dependent upon rather limited social security benefits.

One route that working class and working poor Americans traditionally took in pursuit of a better life was enlisting in the armed services. A period spent either in the US or abroad in the military was useful in obtaining a government job – as a police officer, firefighter, postal carrier and in other relatively lucrative and secure positions. A stint in the Army, Navy, Air Force or Marines typically qualifies one for a preference and a better rank in the queue when roles become available. High school graduates also could go straight into the military and then, through a variety of different schemes, access higher education at a lesser cost and with the aid of their earnings from their time in uniform. Of course, those who enlisted assumed the risk that they could be deployed to fight in a war or to danger zones, but conflicts weren't perpetual and, for obvious political reasons, the use of armed force had been something of a last resort, a necessary evil of sorts. That was before the endless fighting in the Middle East. It commenced in the early 1990s, was arguably unjustified and counterproductive and alternatively took or destroyed hundreds of thousands of American lives – not to mention the devastating effects on enemy combatants in the region and the innocent people they were defending.

Many Americans hail from military families in which successive generations went into the same branch. Grandparents and parents fought in the World Wars, in Korea and Vietnam. They viewed it as a duty to their country and often saw horrific things and performed extraordinary deeds that they seldom, if ever, spoke about again. These patriots did so out of a love for America and were motivated by a deep-rooted faith that they were fighting on the side of moral righteousness and for the greater good.

The experience of the young soldiers who followed their lead was totally different. The explanations proffered for their being sent thousands of miles from home were unclear, at best, and potentially in contravention of international law – tantamount to warmongering – at worst. The ideology of neo-conservatism was favoured by the Bush family and their allies. Neo-conservatives believe that the US should aggressively promote democracy around the world through interventionism. Its influential adherents were aided and abetted by the military-industrial complex. That is where primary responsibility for what ultimately proved to be catastrophic at every level lies.

The repercussions of many years of uninterrupted and unsuccessful conflict were felt directly and indirectly by millions of Americans. What has happened in the Middle East and afterwards at home made lots of them contemplate one question: Why? And in this context it is only natural that, by 2013, more than half of the American people had come around to agreeing with the overtly isolationist proposition that the US should 'mind its own business internationally and let other countries get along the best they can on their own'. Thirty per cent felt that way eleven years previously and a mere eighteen per cent concurred in 1964.[15] The shift is pronounced and rapid.

Meanwhile, a college or university education, long the gateway to economic prosperity, became ever more difficult to access. The costs of the best institutions in the late 20th century, already exorbitant by comparison to the rest of the world, have skyrocketed to the stratosphere. In the early to mid-1990s, tuition at the highest-rated colleges and universities hovered between $20,000 and $30,000. At present, the same

15 Pew Research Center, 'Public Sees US Power Declining as Support for Global Engagement Slips' (3 December 2013) available at https://www.pewresearch. org/politics/2013/12/03/public-sees-u-s-power-declining-as-support-for-global-engagement-slips/ <last accessed 24 June 2021>.

education will run a student and their family in the vicinity of $65,000 annually. There really is no adjective that suffices to describe this inflation.

A tiny sliver, the richest of the rich, the small coterie of winners from the 'new economy' fuelled by technological advances and globalisation, can afford to write these huge cheques for their children and have helped to drive this cost explosion. The institutions defend the colossal rip-off with reference to statistics about return on investment in terms of lifetime earnings and to financial aid packages that discount the actual sum students pay each year. Outside of the Ivy League and a few others, however, so-called 'need blind' financial aid provision that does not take the form of loans is usually confined to top-notch athletes and applicants from minority groups. The truth of the matter is that a great many talented young Americans hold a very good undergraduate degree, oftentimes in a liberal arts discipline that may not lead initially to a living wage, and are crippled by a debt burden in the six figures. That this is so prevalent makes it no less tragic or damning. That neither Democrats nor Republicans have ever sought to rein in this extortion, by tackling it in a meaningful way, is absolutely bizarre. It would be a ready-made political winner. Initiatives to make community colleges and two-year degrees free or affordable are welcomed. They are merely scratching the surface, though, and bolder action is required. And if precedent is any dictate, progress will be glacial.

The confluence of these causes and effects created a rotting stew. They brought about a general air of malaise in the US. Again, politicians have been deterred from doing their business well by the allure of big dollars and attendant special interests. The US Supreme Court, in a 1976 case, *Buckley v Valeo*, deemed money in the form of campaign contributions the equivalent of free speech and hence entitled to expansive 1st Amendment protection. And in 2010, in *Citizens United v Federal Election Commission*, it was decided that the 1st Amendment prohibits restrictions on political communications by corporations, labour unions and other organisations. During that time, as campaign cash became king, Democrats and Republicans ignored the malaise and sought to downplay it. One wonders if their leaders who continued to mouth platitudes about America's best days being ahead of it ever thought of how hollow and nonsensical they must have seemed to an unemployed steelworker or Iraq war veteran struggling with post-traumatic stress disorder. I recall vividly thinking as much on several occasions when President Obama delivered speeches full of soaring, inspirational and impassioned rhetoric. As always, the words sounded wonderful. The speeches still lifted the room. But did they reflect reality for and/or meet the mood of millions who were hurting? Not in my view.

Unable to think beyond the inside baseball that's played in the Washington, DC bubble and the conventional wisdom about the ways things always had been, the establishments of the two parties and their respective apparatchiks must have presumed that the 'system' would prevail and that the two parties would absorb the disaffected within them and these citizens would continue to have to make a binary choice when they went to the polls. Politicians within each party would nod in their direction – Republicans through cultural conservatism and Democrats through populist rhetoric on the economy – and votes would be cast on that basis. This constituency of Americans would trend more Republican as time went by, yet their departure from the erstwhile home in the Democratic Party would be offset by the drift of some in the professional classes, women in particular, away from the GOP, as well as the allegiance of the growing Latino community. The status quo would be adjusted, though not upended. Indeed, in the latter half of the Obama presidency, a widespread view in the DC commentariat was that another Bush, Jeb, the former Florida governor, would become the Republican presidential nominee in 2016.

Because they were so out of touch, they failed to apprehend what was coming. They had seen Buchanan and Perot attempt to capture the presidency on the basis of long-simmering resentment and frustration and fail miserably. But things had reached a near boiling point after two terms of Barack Obama, having been sparked further by the flames of racial prejudice. What's more, the top Republicans spectacularly failed to perceive the growing disconnect between their traditional conservative ideology and what their grassroots actually believed. They widely misunderstood the Tea Party as a coalition of far-right individuals who were ultra-committed disciples of right-wing dogma and wanted it carried to extreme ends. Destroy Obamacare. Kill off government programmes and bloated bureaucracy. Show how committed Republicans are to ending unnecessary spending by shutting down the government if needs be. This is not what most animated what became of the Tea Party. In my view, it was, instead, a loud and angry manifestation of the 'turn back the clock' conservatism that had gained currency within the GOP. Whether they knew and accepted it or not, the elected officials had lost control.

One cunning person grasped all of this. He saw the incongruous, complicated, seemingly contradictory, frightening and downright odd milieu that I have endeavoured to outline and saw a path to power. He recognised that a vast swathe of Americans loathed politics and politicians and were far more enthralled by popular culture, reality TV and social media than the 'same old, same old' they heard from Republicans and Democrats alike. He knew that, if he could get a spot on the same stage with a large group of buttoned-up, programmed, establishment-oriented Republican figures and say something different, he would stand out and have a chance at winning the presidential nomination. Because he is such an egotist and in possession of unparalleled self-belief, he imagined that, if he could pull off that feat, presumptive Democratic nominee Hillary Clinton was so disdained by enough Americans of every stripe that they would cast a ballot for him as the lesser of two evils and he could become an improbable President of the United States – critics be damned.

Enter Donald J. Trump.

CHAPTER 20

The Trump Presidency

When the rumours began circulating in 2015 that the bombastic New York billionaire, Donald Trump, was considering a bid for the presidency, I was dismissive. I even recall saying on the radio that he was only floating the possibility to enhance his brand and that, if the convert to conservatism did attempt such a quixotic quest, he would not even feature in the contest for the Republican nomination. Indeed, Donald Trump, who embodied the excesses of the 1980s and was discovered by a new generation as the star of *The Apprentice*, had expressed this ambition in the past and flirted more than once with mounting a candidacy. Like lots of other political watchers, I chuckled when I watched the spectacle of paid attendees at Trump Tower in Manhattan clapping wildly when he announced his intention to go through with it in mid-June of 2015. One news outlet promptly stated that Trump's campaign would be covered solely in its entertainment, and not in its news, section. Perversely, from its editorial point of view, that originally principled decision probably helped aid Trump's pursuit of power.

Most eyes turned to the strong field of approximately 16 other contenders. Whether one agrees or disagrees with their politics, it was comprised of capable men and women with considerable experience in elected office as members of the US Senate and House of Representatives, as governors and mayors, and some with backgrounds as high-ranking executives in global corporations. A lot of them got in the race because they believed that, when push came to shove, ostensible favourite Jeb Bush would not be up to it. Each sketched out a plausible scenario in which he or she would be the one left standing when Bush fell. The front runners in the large pack were Bush, Texas Senator Ted Cruz, Florida Senator Marco Rubio and Ohio Governor John Kasich. Their ideologies and dispositions were indistinguishable. But rather shockingly, the opinion polls consistently put Donald Trump right with them in the upper echelon. In the early stages, pundits – I was one – attributed this to name recognition and novelty and predicted confidently that Trump would fade by the time the candidates were criss-crossing frozen corn fields in Iowa and sitting down to breakfast in no-frills diners in Manchester, New Hampshire.

But he didn't. In every televised debate, Trump stood out in the crowd – both by what he was saying, much of which deviated 'big league' from conservative principles, and in how he said it, in his own inimitable style. Portraying himself as a non-politician who would bring a businessman's outlook to governance worked to his advantage. And despite the collective revulsion of right-wing intellectuals at his apostasies on the virtues of global trade and the free market, as well as America's role in the world, it turns out that there was a very receptive audience for what he was saying. And notwithstanding his being narrowly bested in the Iowa caucus by Ted Cruz –

who sagely sewed doubt there about the sincerity of Trump's conversion to the pro-life cause among the older evangelical Christians who are a major political force in the Hawkeye State – Trump benefitted repeatedly as the orthodox Republicans divvied up the votes of like-minded party members across the country. What had been unthinkable came to pass and he won the GOP presidential nomination to the chagrin of the senior figures and the establishment, some of whom quite publicly voiced their displeasure with the result.

On the other side, the woman who everyone thought would coast to victory, Hillary Clinton, managed to outlast the self-described socialist and curmudgeonly Vermont Senator, Bernie Sanders. That Sanders' insurgent candidacy proved so difficult to overcome for the former Secretary of State, New York Senator and First Lady was still another symptom of American malaise, albeit from the hard left in this instance. Clinton was undeniably damaged by the unanticipated, draining primary duel. Moreover, whatever its myriad causes, the hatred (no other word suffices) for Hillary Clinton was broader and deeper in the electorate than anyone could have imagined. Donald Trump could not have picked a better foe. And he wasted no time in going on the attack. 'Crooked Hillary' was his constant refrain and he used it to great effect.

That said, and despite Clinton's unpopularity and other political weaknesses, Trump was the clear underdog. Every way I looked at the Electoral College map and every time I conceived of the best possible result for the Republican, I still couldn't envisage a navigable channel to the 270 votes necessary to prevail. But those of us who just didn't think

Trump could win had no idea that Clinton would run a total stinker of a campaign. Of course, some analysts have posited that FBI Director James Comey effectively denied her the presidency when he sent a letter to Congress just a week prior to the election indicating that emails pertinent to the investigation of her use of a private email server as Secretary of State in the Obama administration had been discovered. That certainly didn't help, yet bad news strikes almost every political campaign and, as in this instance, the what, when, where and how lie beyond the control of the candidate and the strategists. It's a fact of life in the business.

Hillary Clinton and her team made two egregious errors, which, in my opinion, were the dispositive factors in her losing what had been deemed an 'unlosable' election. First, it is widely known that the greatest instinctual politician of my lifetime, Bill Clinton, on his travels in Middle America to appeal to people to rally behind his wife and take the temperature on the ground, saw that there was a problem. There was an unmistakable groundswell of enthusiasm for Donald Trump, some of which was palpable in territory that Democrats should own. In Michigan, in particular, where no Republican had won since George HW Bush in 1988, he sensed that Hillary was in trouble. The story is that he went back to campaign headquarters in New York and apprised the staffers of his assessment and was swiftly rebuffed because what he was telling them didn't align with the data and algorithms being relied upon. Regardless of whether that was how matters actually unfolded or not, it was an obscenely bad plan to take states like Michigan and Wisconsin for granted and to indulge in premature fantasies about flipping once solidly red states whose demographics were shifting.

Second, there was Clinton's oddly deliberate slip of the tongue in September when she uttered the following words:

> You know, to just be grossly generalistic, you could put half of Trump's supporters into what I call the basket of deplorables. Right? They're racist, sexist, homophobic, xenophobic, Islamophobic – you name it. And unfortunately, there are people like that. And he has lifted them up. He has given voice to their websites that used to only have 11,000 people – now have 11 million. He tweets and retweets their offensive, hateful, mean-spirited rhetoric. Now, some of those folks – they are irredeemable, but thankfully, they are not America.

Was she right in that some Trump voters harbour such views? Yes, and more recent events confirm it. The perception that her comments would give rise to was obvious, however: she stood in condescending judgement of millions of hurting Americans. Many of them already had their doubts about the incredibly wealthy Clintons; others hadn't made up their minds definitively. She was one of the hated elites. It is probable that her remarks alienated working-class white women especially and pushed them in Trump's direction. That they emerged from a glitzy LGBT fundraiser in Manhattan made the optics even worse.

Nonetheless, I remained sceptical that Trump could manage an upset because the Electoral College map was so stacked against him. Yet thanks to his opponent's haplessness as an office seeker, it became possible that a man she correctly said 'lacked the temperament to be President of the United States' could do it. And on the night, things broke in his direction. It is no overstatement to say that he shocked the world. In the immediate aftermath of the political earthquake, reactions could be divided into two broad camps. One was rather apocalyptic, positing that a Trump presidency posed an existential threat to American democracy and imperilled the world. The other, where I was firmly planted, was that the US would weather the storm just fine, that some of his foes were getting carried away in their dire proclamations as to what was in store and that Trump might surprise us and govern differently than he had campaigned. Reflecting back on the four years in the White House he was granted by the electorate, the truth was somewhere in the middle, but closer to the former school of thought than the latter.

Indeed, President Trump's inaugural address pulled no punches and was followed swiftly by moves to ban the entry of people from a number of predominantly Muslim countries from entering the US and to construct a wall on the southern border. The talk of building a wall wasn't merely a metaphor for tightening immigration laws, after all. The ugly rhetoric was followed up by concerted action. Activists on the left were immediately mobilised and took to the streets to fight back against a man they saw as a would-be fascist dictator. His unfortunate statement in 2017, after a violent riot instigated by white supremacists at a 'Unite the Right' rally in Charlottesville, Virginia, that there were 'fine people on both sides' of the skirmishes there further inflamed opposition to him. That he refused to back down from it when given the opportunity and when the details of that sorry day were laid bare was objectively appalling.

On the flip side, his backers were heartened at what they saw as Donald Trump bucking the trend and living up to the pledges that he made. Cutting taxes and remaking the US federal judiciary in accordance with the wishes of religious conservatives were core elements of his agenda. What's more, at his boisterous and well-attended rallies, he touted other accomplishments, such as bringing more manufacturing jobs home and keeping the US out of foreign wars. He asserted that he was making America great again and putting America first, as he had promised. And the economic indicators were very favourable for most of his tenure.

That said, the issues and the problems facing the US took a back seat much of the time as Trump's presidency was overshadowed by the circus-like sideshows and assorted controversies that emanated from it. Of these, the Mueller investigation into Russian interference in the 2016 presidential election and links between Trump associates and Russian officials was the most significant. At various moments while it was ongoing, Trump's enemies showed that they were willing to latch onto anything damning of the president without making any effort to ascertain whether the latest revelation had any basis in the facts or the evidence. Trump was naturally dismissive of it. It wasn't long before the Americans who matter most politically – those in the middle – had tuned out and didn't pay it much heed.

Ultimately, the Mueller Report in 2019 found that the

Russians had interfered with the election and that Trump's team realised that their man would benefit. But the investigation 'did not establish that members of the Trump campaign conspired or coordinated with the Russian government in its election interference activities'. The report was an exoneration, albeit a partial one, for the president and he continued to portray himself as a victim of a hyper-partisan witch hunt. Later in the year, Democrats in the House of Representatives impeached President Trump. In the main, it was for allegedly seeking a quid pro quo from the Ukrainian president Volodymyr Zelensky: if Zelensky held a probe into the past, purportedly nefarious dealings of Joe Biden and his son Hunter in the country, then Trump would release millions in military aid to Ukraine. There was no smoking gun, however, and never any chance of the required two-thirds of the membership of the US Senate opting to convict the president and remove him from office. It may seem strange to gloss over the Mueller Report and an impeachment, but neither wounded him badly. In fact, both only heightened enthusiasm among his base. Democrats, prodded by a vocal left flank that smelled blood in the water, allowed the disdain in their hearts for the president to rule their heads and put far too much stock in what the report and impeachment could deliver.

In early 2020, as the Democratic aspirants fought it out over who would take him on, there was ample cause for optimism in the Trump universe. Sure, there were plenty of Americans who despised him, who couldn't stomach the prospect that he might have four more years as commander-in-chief, freed from any electoral constraints. But he also was in firm possession of an enviable critical mass of disciples who adored him and would show up at the polling place come hell or high water for their man. And the key reason for feeling good was that the crucial indicators in terms of Americans' collective financial health were solid. The economy was robust. For example, the rate of unemployment among historically disadvantaged racial minorities was at an all-time low. Then COVID-19 hit and changed the equation.

President Trump's first response was to deny the pandemic and play down its significance. Then, when its impact started to be felt broadly and wasn't amenable to being wished away, he panicked. He knew that coronavirus had instantly become a large obstacle to his re-election chances because of its public health implications, on the one hand, and the economic harm it would do, on the other. The sales pitch he had ready for the small coterie of Americans who didn't have strong feelings about him one way or another – 'you might not like me, but look at your wallet or pocketbook' – would not have the same resonance. He was extremely foolish not to expressly say at the outset that, in battling COVID, his administration planned to follow in almost every respect the advice of public health experts like Dr Anthony Fauci.

Doing so could hardly have been assailed in the sense that he would have appeared to be taking a responsible course of action and listening to the people who know best during an unprecedented crisis that was afflicting countless Americans. Moreover, from a raw political point of view, following the dictates, more or less, of Dr Fauci and others may have provided the president with a layer of insulation from people's anger and outrage about what had come to pass at so many levels. Trump could have acknowledged that he understood how difficult things were for millions of Americans, yet insist that the top priority had to be saving lives and the doctors were the ones who knew best how to do that.

Naturally, that may have disappointed some elements of his base, but it is unlikely that they would have deserted him because they didn't have anywhere else to turn. Moreover, letting Dr Fauci take the lead would have reassured men and women over 65, the most reliable voters and the cohort of the electorate that had put him over the top in 2016. Instead, driven by his outsized ego and insatiable thirst to always be at the centre of things, he held ridiculous nightly press conferences in which he regularly contradicted the experts, sent mixed messages and delegated authority to local government, effectively creating a patchwork quilt of incoherent rules and regulations around the country. The administration's response to COVID-19 was undeniably slow and ineffectual, given the astonishing amount of cases and deaths. It is likely that many more people got sick and died than should have as a result.

In hindsight, the pandemic was probably fatal to President Trump's hopes for a second term. To indulge a hypothetical, had it not surfaced and had the economy kept ticking along, the chances are that he would have prevailed. Back in the real world, if the administration reacted to COVID by pivoting aggressively to keep people safe, Trump would still have been in a good position. On the latter point, the exit polls show that the president's support was down 2–3% among older voters, the segment most concerned about coronavirus and disenchanted by Trump's mishandling of it. Given the relatively slim margin by which he lost the election, had he held onto these voters, there is a strong chance he would have won again.

Another point worth noting is that the murder of George Floyd by Minneapolis police officer Derek Chauvin in May of 2020 was burned into the nation's collective consciousness. It spurred people of colour into action on many fronts. One of these was political activism. They mobilised and turned out in big numbers in key states for Democratic candidates up and down the ballot who were much more sympathetic to their calls for policing reform and a recalibration of the relationship between law enforcement and young African-American males.

Even accepting the pandemic and his administration's inexcusable bungling of it, as well as the overdue reckoning with race and racism, I don't believe that Trump was truly finished until the first presidential debate with his rival, Joe Biden. Everyone knew that Trump would be fired up, argumentative and potentially outrageous. He surpassed himself on all three fronts. The president said that smart was not a word that should be associated with Biden who, he claimed, had finished last in his college class. Additionally, when the former vice-president mentioned the sadness he experienced on the death from brain cancer of his son Beau, Trump responded disgracefully in declining to express sympathy and by making a nasty comment about Biden's other son, Hunter, who has long battled drug addiction and personal demons.

His conduct in that debate revealed more about the quality of the man. In fact, the attack on Hunter Biden was just plain dumb. Literally millions of parents in the US, many of whom are struggling financially and otherwise and voted for Donald Trump in 2016, have children with similar problems who they love and would do anything to help. It was heartless, demonstrated a total lack of empathy and almost certainly convinced lots of citizens in Middle America, women in particular, that the man born into wealth and privilege did not deserve their vote. This was also a major contributing factor to Trump's defeat: enough Americans had seen enough of him and yearned for a different, calmer period.

In this regard, Joe Biden was the ideal foil for Donald Trump. And after flirting with several of his opponents in the Democratic primary, including Bernie Sanders for a second time, I am convinced that, whether they did so consciously or subconsciously, Democrats recognised that Biden was best placed to topple the president and fell in line behind him, notwithstanding their misgivings about the elderly native of Scranton, Pennsylvania. His shortcomings as a politician aside, Biden deserves a tremendous amount of credit for triumphing over adversity so many times in his very public life – from losing his first wife and young daughter in a car accident decades ago, to being humiliated in his first quest for the Oval Office in 1988, to surviving two brain aneurysms, to the death in 2015 of his son who had followed him into politics. He kept going and eventually won the prize he had his eye on forever.

Watching the final days of the campaign, I was fairly convinced that Trump could not win the presidency. I ran the Electoral College numbers over and over again and could not reach any conclusion other than that Biden would win. Therein lay my sole hesitation about calling it definitely: I had done the very same four years previously and saw no path to victory for Trump. I was extremely confident then that Hillary Clinton would prevail. Just prior to the 2020 election, this lingering misgiving was intensified by my sense that Trump had clawed back some support among older voters by exploiting fears on the issue of race and by caricaturing the Democrats as very far left. This was reflected in tightening polls in Pennsylvania. The Biden team clearly was worried, too, as it sent the man who was born there and who local sympathetic pollsters had been very optimistic about to the state on the weekend before Election Day. Against this creeping feeling, there were also the thoughts that Joe Biden was much better liked than Hillary Clinton and that a lot of Americans were through with President Trump.

Biden did hang on. And even though Trump delivered a ridiculous speech to supporters in the wee hours of Wednesday, 4 November, and continued to assert vociferously with no evidence that he had won the election, I thought that it was the end – that he would leave, not as a gentleman, but that he would go quietly. It turns out that there was one more unsettling surprise in store.

January 6, 2021 will go down as one of the lowest points in American history. A crowd of several thousand men and women – protesters who morphed into a group of rioters, looters and, arguably, domestic terrorists – descended upon Washington, DC in planes, trains, buses and private cars from all over the US. They came to the capital city on the day that Congress was to ratify the verdict of the Electoral College that Joe Biden and Kamala Harris would be the next president and vice-president to put everyone on notice that they did not accept the outcome of the election on November 3rd.

That mayhem and chaos lay ahead should have been clear from social media activity and from the fashion in which several of them menacingly confronted Mitt Romney in a Utah airport lounge and then shouted abuse at him on the plane they flew on together. That morning, the radicalised Trump adherents were addressed by Rudy Giuliani, by Donald Trump Jr and by the president himself. President Trump told them that his 'election victory was stolen by emboldened radical left Democrats … and the fake news media' and, after riling them up with a pack of lies about stolen votes and widespread election fraud, concluded: 'We're going to walk down Pennsylvania Avenue … we're going to the Capitol and we're going to try and give our Republicans … the kind of pride and boldness that they need to take back our country.'

What transpired subsequently – the physical desecration of the seat of American democracy and the deaths of five individuals, including a Capitol police officer – unfolded in front of a rapt global television audience. President Trump, his immediate family and their inner circle of sycophants held something of a 'watch party' on the grounds of the White House that made its way onto social media and at which their glee and jubilation after the crowd had been whipped up into a frenzy were sickeningly manifest.

Taking it all in, I was consumed more by sadness than by anger or outrage at the sight of images I never thought I would see. In truth, this was the apotheosis of a poisonous and fractious political culture that has changed dramatically for the worse in a relatively short timeframe.

Looking back, Biden won the Democratic nomination on his third try in large part because there was one impulse that animated his party's grassroots above all: it was imperative to end the Trump presidency. He was – correctly, in my estimation – seen as the man for the job. That said, the primary fight did highlight internal ideological and related discord, which has been framed as the insurgent progressive wing against the moderate establishment wing. On the other side, the GOP is also described as riven and in the throes of a 'civil war' between Trump loyalists and mainstream conservatives like Congresswoman Liz Cheney, whose father was George W. Bush's vice-president.

Yet again, these black and white portrayals of the power struggles within the two parties are gross oversimplifications. In truth, in 2021, Republicans and Democrats alike have rather unique challenges and opportunities. That their proverbial glasses are half-full in one sense and half-empty in another stems from the upending of American politics that Donald Trump's stint in charge was equally a symptom of and a catalyst for. The current, strange state of play makes it nigh on impossible to provide a coherent appraisal of what the future may bring. Here goes anyway.

CHAPTER 21

The Future of American Politics

When looked at from afar, with the benefits of distance and detachment, it is objectively bizarre that there are only two major political parties in the US. It is a vast nation that takes in rural and urban locales, densely and sparsely populated areas, landlocked and coastal states, cold and warm climate zones, flat and mountainous terrain, islands in the Pacific Ocean and territory in the Arctic Circle. Its approximately 330,000,000 inhabitants are diverse in every conceivable way. To illustrate this truism, as a native of the Boston area, I would guarantee that I have more in common with contemporaries who were born and raised in Ireland than with someone from rural Idaho or the Deep South. We may all be Americans, but the country we know, identify with and love is often a very different place.

How then can two political parties possibly say that they can represent all of the interests of these people and geographic regions when they inherently diverge? Critics of American democracy have a fast answer: they can't. It is not a question that a great many Americans spend any time considering, so engrained is the two-party system in our shared consciousness. Democrats and Republicans have for some time cynically colluded in what is a mutually beneficial arrangement. The institutional obstacles to a third party's establishment and lasting relevance, which they have helped to create, are enormous.

The most successful in recent memory was Ross Perot's Reform Party, which he utilised his virtually unlimited resources to create as a vehicle for his second, initially promising presidential run in 1996. The Commission on Presidential Debates, sponsored jointly by Republicans and Democrats, had other ideas, however, and changed the rules to exclude him from participating in the debates. Perot won 8% of the vote. That, together with the 1998 election of the professional wrestler turned Governor of Minnesota, Jesse 'The Body' Ventura, was the party's high-water mark. Pat Buchanan hitched his wagon to it briefly and Donald Trump pondered joining, but in-fighting was rife, its raison d'être vanished and now there are just a few thousand members left. The other parties in America most commonly mentioned, the Greens and the Libertarians, have less than a million members between them.

So again, how can the parties claim to be natural homes for individuals who are so different that they will inevitably disagree on lots of important issues? The historic answer offered by the leading Democrats and Republicans has been that theirs are 'big tents' – that they are united by several overarching principles, but that there are areas where people are not prohibited from dissenting on what may feature in the party platform. And for those who have championed the notion that the parties should be big tents, having a heterogeneous composition is not a weakness. It is a strength. To them, political parties should not be akin to cults in demanding unwavering fidelity on every topic without exception. They are necessarily broad and welcoming coalitions. Indeed, making a party a big tent is also politically expedient in that it engenders the chance for parties to be competitive and elect candidates in jurisdictions where aspects of party dogma are anathema.

In the past, this school of thought was prevalent, near-universal. During the latter half of the twentieth century, the Republican Party became more conservative and the Democratic Party shifted to the left. Nonetheless, there were numerous centrist to liberal Republican elected officials at all levels, particularly in the north-eastern US. They tended to be 'hands off' on social issues, which they insisted was consistent with their being fiscally prudent advocates for small government. Conversely, there was still a not inconsiderable cadre of socially conservative, economically populist Democrats, mainly southerners or mid-westerners who were uncomfortable leaving the party they had always belonged to, as well as the ethnic Catholics concentrated in and around large American cities such as Boston, Chicago, New York and Philadelphia. Those at the top of the parties accepted and listened respectfully to their rebel voices in recognition of the fact that toeing the party line would in all likelihood cost them a seat. The big-money donors, however, emphatically did not adopt a similarly sympathetic stance and were appalled by the thought that their dollars could be used to shore up a politician whose positions on 'hot button' matters they found abhorrent.

'Money talks' is the golden rule in American politics. Accordingly, there has been a purge and elected moderates have become an endangered species in both parties. Arguably, though, the Republicans have done a better job of facilitating moderates than the Democrats. For instance, Charlie Baker and Phil Scott, the governors of Massachusetts and Vermont, steadfast blue states with hard-left congressional delegations, are liberal Republicans who openly criticise the policies and take issue with the ideological trajectory of the national party. Both stated publicly that they did not vote for Donald Trump. There are plenty of other like-minded GOP elected personnel – Maine Senator Susan Collins has the highest profile – throughout the New England states.

Meanwhile, middle-of-the-road Democrats are relatively fewer and farther between. Governor John Bel Edwards of Louisiana and Senator Joe Manchin of West Virginia are two of the last around. More typical is the example of former Congressman Collin Peterson. The long-serving incumbent from Minnesota was scorned by insurgent progressives for opposing abortion and gun control and for voting against the first impeachment of President Trump. Peterson was also an ardent backer of farmers and a champion of workers' rights. In 2020, he was defeated by a right-wing Republican, who advantageously linked him to his liberal colleagues in the House of Representatives.

In short, and regardless of the protestations to the contrary that leading Republicans and Democrats might offer, the parties' tents have shrunk, primarily at the behest of moneyed special interests who increasingly dictate the political strategy and the ordering of priorities. At the same time, they have to be acutely aware that 'Trumpism' – or what I have sketched out more amorphously as a third way – is a force to be reckoned with. There is a substantial audience that has come to reject the orthodoxies of both parties. The question is: how do Democrats and Republicans go about winning over the hearts and minds of the 74 million Americans who cast ballots in favour of the 45th president's re-election and loads more who sympathised with elements of the message, but could not bring themselves to endorse the narcissistic messenger?

It may seem odd to suggest that these Americans are 'gettable' for the Democratic Party. But that is only if one fully accepts the narrative that the citizenry is hopelessly divided into blue and red camps. Again, it appears that way because the voters have a binary choice on the ballot paper. In reality, Democrats could claw back a lot of these men and women, enough to win elections in all 50 states, if they changed emphasis and opened their tent ever so slightly. Embracing the economic populism that propelled Bernie Sanders to national prominence and earned him a dedicated following is one key aspect of it. Scepticism about trade deals; a demonstrated commitment to preserving what's left of manufacturing and to retraining those who have been displaced; a concerted focus on raising the minimum wage and on good pay levels for all; making third-level education more affordable and expanding access to healthcare are the core components. The majority of Americans, especially those in Middle America whose support the Democrats need most, would nod right along in agreement with these aims.

Straightforward talking points on 'bread and butter' issues that matter above everything else to ordinary individuals and families should be front and centre. Simultaneously, and without abandoning their liberal ideals, the party should endeavour to erase the common perception that it is more dedicated to doing the bidding of their well-heeled coastal benefactors and powerful forces in the culture wars than to people who work with their hands and live pay cheque to pay cheque. It could do so by amending some of the uncompromising language in the platform and by fostering an open environment that does not repel those who oppose abortion or own guns or are somewhat uncomfortable with the rapidly changing landscape in their country. Additionally, the party would have to rediscover the anti-war, anti-interventionist spirit that once animated it. If the Democrats went in this direction, I am convinced that the party would enjoy extraordinary electoral victories and soon occupy an overwhelming preponderance of political offices at federal, state and local levels. They have a tremendous opportunity.

But I would bet that they won't avail of it. There is little chance of the party pivoting determinedly in this fashion because of the stranglehold leftist special interests have on it and because of its growing dependency on super-wealthy corporations and individuals as the once-robust labour union movement has deteriorated into a shadow of its former self. It appears set to traipse on, as handicapped as it is bolstered by the course it has charted. The party will justifiably assert that the horizon is bright in some respects, given that its gains among the college-educated professional class, having been put off by the GOP's social conservatism and by Donald

Trump's persona, have made it competitive in states and districts that it used to write off. The astonishing victories of liberal Democrats in run-off elections for the US Senate in once deep-red Georgia is a standout example and a genuine source for optimism, even if conservatives are right to cite some distinguishing characteristics of those races. And furthermore, Democrats point to the changing demographics in the US and the forecast that people of colour will constitute the majority of the population in decades to come. This, it had been postulated, would be the guarantor of a Democratic future. Recent voting patterns and polling trends, though, suggest that demographics may not be destiny after all.

An unforeseeable opening for the Republicans lies therein. I consider the biggest story of the 2020 election neither to be the vanquishing of Donald Trump nor the Democrats' barely retaking control of the US Senate. Rather, it is the growing support for the Republican Party among Hispanic or Latino Americans. Depending on which set of data one deems most reliable, somewhere between 34% and 40% of Latinos cast ballots for Donald Trump and other conservatives on the ballot. This defied the conventional wisdom to the effect that, because of race-baiting techniques utilised by the Republicans, Latinos would be not much different than African Americans and vote for Democrats en masse. There is no doubt that Democrats eagerly bought into this reasoning – in particular when Trump advocated building a wall on the southern border with Mexico and labelled undocumented immigrants who made their way into the US 'criminals' and 'rapists' – and have neglected their efforts to reach out to and cultivate the support of the fastest-growing bloc of voters in the country. Some party members are still in denial, owing to a regrettable refusal to accept that many Latinos think differently about what are articles of faith for the left, but the Democratic Party has a very serious problem it needs to get to grips with.

Religious and community leaders identify three factors for the fact that Latinos are not a monolithic grouping in their political leanings. First, many fled to the US because of the socialist regimes in their native countries which were corrupt and responsible for human rights abuses, dire poverty and a dearth of prospects for a better life. The Republican tarring of Democratic policies as 'socialist' brings back dreadful memories and is a very persuasive tactic. Second, Latinos are far more religious than other groupings. Their Catholicism or evangelical Christianity informs their staunch pro-life convictions and an unapologetically traditionalist disposition. They are appalled by what they see as the Democrats' abandonment of people whose moral compass is informed by their religious faith. Third, there is a burgeoning class of successful small business owners and second- and third-generation professionals who favour the Republican low-tax economic model. In short, the early indicators of the trajectory of their American assimilation suggest that, in time, Latino Americans may be more like Irish-Americans – some of whom are accused of 'pulling up the ladder behind them' – than African Americans in their political allegiances. That is, they will be diffuse: right, left and centre. If this transpires, it alters the long-anticipated and widely forecast political dynamics fundamentally. Asian Americans should be watched in this regard, too.

And if Republicans temper Trump's rhetoric around immigration – not switching to an avowedly pro-immigration posture, but emphasising that there is a welcome mat for those who are willing to work hard and play by the rules – I see no reason why they can't make deeper inroads so long as the Democrats stay the course and do not respond adequately to what they hear from Latinos. Of course, Republicans cannot afford to excessively favour a permissive immigration regime lest they alienate the segment of the population that is now their base: white people who do not hold a college or university degree.

Exit polls in recent elections without exception have shown that around two-thirds of them vote Republican and that this solidified after the Obama presidency and during Trump's tenure. This cohort had been roughly equally spread between Republicans and Democrats, but flocked to the GOP as, concurrently, labour unions shrunk in size and influence and Democrats no longer felt it necessary to follow their lead. The Democrats' leftward lurch on 'God, guns and guts' was also a huge contributor in their departure. Moreover, despite some not insignificant haemorrhaging, there is a large chunk of college-educated, well-to-do white voters who remain solidly Republican, their misgivings about the influence of evangelicals and Trump's apparent takeover notwithstanding.

In sum, even though the big tents have shrunk, it very much appears that the parties will continue to have to rely on unwieldy coalitions of groups with competing interests in order to win elections. Democrats can depend to varying extents on people of colour, the young, LGBT activists and allies, highly educated, culturally liberal, forward-thinking white professionals and must do their best to at least get the white working class to hear them out. The Republicans can generally count on the white working class, wealthy individuals and big corporations whose primary desire is to minimise their tax liabilities, a substantial cadre of Latinos (and also some Asian Americans). They must seek to peel off whoever else they can. Were it not for the design of the founding fathers – the Electoral College system in which the popular vote is secondary, a US Senate with two representatives from each state regardless of its size – as well as adroit manoeuvring by Republicans on devising the boundaries of districts in the House of Representatives, the wind would be with the Democrats. That is not the case and they must operate within a structure that is not amenable to being torn down and rebuilt, unfair as they may decry it to be.

This is all very messy and muddled. A lot of the old absolutes have been dented or demolished. And it is incredibly hard to sound coherent when taking the long view of American politics, which seems destined to be inescapably incoherent. If the American polity was truly polarised, a cogent analysis would be far easier to proffer. But it's not a neat red vs blue, right vs left split; the two-party system just makes it look that way. Instead, it's splintered, and that renders the situation infinitely more complex and less amenable to speak with any degree of certainty about.

Of course, politicians seldom have the luxury of taking such a long view. And in the short term, there are more immediate challenges to be confronted. Republicans must deal with the fallout from the Trump presidency. The astute among them know that Trump has redefined what it means to be a conservative. America First, Make America Great Again or 'turn back the clock' – whichever way it is caricatured – is clearly a better reflection of the thinking of the faithful on the ground and it has won them new converts. The 74 million votes Trump won, notwithstanding four years of non-stop tumult and damaging controversy, speak for themselves. Leading Republicans may have been sickened by what happened on Capitol Hill in early January of 2021. It may make grappling with the thorny topic of Trump and his family and the cult of personality that has sprung up around them a little easier, but they still haven't gone away.

While there is not much that can be said definitively about Donald Trump's future and allowing for the fact that he has an unparalleled capacity to surprise to the consternation of his foes, his conduct that day and subsequent second impeachment may mean that he is a force who won't loom quite as large as he would have otherwise. Ideally, Republicans would adopt and adapt elements of Trump's message, but put the man and his family in the rear-view mirror. If they cannot, it will ultimately prove distracting and detrimental. At any rate, it will be fascinating to see how the post-Trump GOP manages this high-wire balancing act in its dealings with the Biden administration and how its 2024 presidential aspirants compete against this backdrop. It is important to be mindful that Donald Trump himself is down, though it would be premature to say that he is out; on the other hand, Trumpism is alive, well and potent.

Having witnessed the loss and other travails of former President Trump, leftist Democrats are buoyed and press the case that they need to act aggressively to implement their agenda and to counteract the myriad misdeeds that were executed during his tenure. Against that, the verdict of the American people was not as unambiguous as has been claimed. Democrats lost seats in the House of Representatives and were wiped out at state and local level. One operative called the underperformance a 'huge catastrophe' and others were equally downbeat. President Biden, who started his career as a centrist and slowly, expediently gravitated leftward, would do well to summon up his old instincts. To be sure, there are elements on the progressives' wish list that can and should be put near the top, such as improving upon aspects of Obamacare and making higher education more accessible, but the culture wars should be approached with abundant caution.

For campaigning in the US never relents. There will be mid-term elections in 2022 and they will be a referendum on the Biden presidency in many respects. The efficacy of his administration's response to COVID-19, both as regards public health and the economy, could be decisive. Its impact has been positive and he and his party are benefitting thus far in the polls. President Biden managed to get a $1.9 trillion COVID-relief package through Congress without a single Republican vote. In addition, his efforts to accomplish something that his predecessor falsely said he would do are commendable: bring members of Congress together and negotiate a comprehensive plan to rebuild America's crumbling infrastructure. This would put millions of men and women back to work and reap far-reaching political dividends. Biden's many years in the Senate and sterling reputation have been a help to the causes he is staking his presidency on. His first 100 days were a success. The more stuff he can get done, the more he can trumpet that he understands 'the art of the deal'. The Republicans' central line of attack, no matter what, will be that Biden may dress up as a moderate, but is a puppet of his party's most strident liberals. The thing is, many ordinary members of the GOP – lots of whom have disavowed what were once articles of faith for conservatives – actually back big government programmes and mammoth expenditures in 2021.

There are pitfalls to be avoided and which Republicans are only too eager to pounce on. At a personal level, as a Democrat of the old school, it is my sincerest hope that President Biden doesn't heed the demands of the hard left in and around the culture wars. That's where we lose. Individuals in Congress and interest groups will lobby his administration constantly to act upon this agenda and exhort their energised adherents to agitate on the streets. I think pushing for the fulfilment of their aspirations ahead of more immediately pressing concerns would harm him and our party politically and should be left to his successor as the face of the Democrats. She or he will surely take them up. I just don't believe that this is the mandate that Joe Biden was given by the American people. Crucially, I believe the key constituency in the electorate – those in the middle, some of them the men and women of Middle America who took a chance on Donald Trump and whose politics are of the third way that I have outlined – gave the senior statesman their endorsement because they trust him to steer the country away from division and with an eye to building consensus, both at home and abroad.

President Biden stressed the theme of unity as the country faces into multiple challenges all at once in his inaugural address. It was the best speech I have ever heard him deliver and one of the finest ever inaugural addresses – memorably delivered at the Capitol Building where, two weeks earlier, radicalised followers of another president had done physical violence to that sacred edifice and to our country's democratic ideals in the process. President Biden is not a transformative political leader. I have been critical of him previously and expect that I will continue to be. There is no way he can fix all that ails the US, a place so many of us in Ireland love dearly and are worried about. In fairness, no one could. But at this trying moment in history, I believe Joe Biden is the best man for an impossible task.

CHAPTER 22

Revitalising the Sacred Transatlantic Relationship

Joe Biden is, depending on how one sees it, either the quintessential or the stereotypical Irish-American. In a 1987 interview with Niall O'Dowd for *Irish-America* magazine, the then-44-year-old US Senator from Delaware described himself very proudly as Irish and a product of an Irish section of Scranton, Pennsylvania. He also spoke about the commitment to Irish issues he had demonstrated from the beginning of his public life. Yet he was less than certain about where in Ireland his roots were.

In response to a question about his ancestral connections by O'Dowd, Biden answered that 'My mother's maiden name was Finnegan; I believe her family was from Mayo. She was one of five children. Her grandfather and grandmother on both sides of the family were 100 percent Irish. The Finnegans came over after the first famine, around 1845. The other members of the extended family all came in that period through to about 1880.'

In the intervening years, it was ascertained that one of his great-great-grandfathers, Patrick Blewitt, was indeed born in

Ballina, County Mayo and made the voyage across the Atlantic in 1850. His other great-great-grandfather, Owen Finnegan, was from the Cooley Peninsula in Louth, where Biden's great-grandfather James Finnegan was also born, and the family emigrated from the wee county to the US in the late 1840s.

Biden has since established a warm kinship with the Blewitts living in Ballina and with his distant cousins in Louth, including the well-known rugby player Rob Kearney. His background as a descendant of famine-era immigrants to the new world is one he shared in common with countless Americans who have been remarkable in the sense that they have excelled in every imaginable area of endeavour. Of course, these Irish Catholics joined many others from the Scots-Irish Protestant tradition who had arrived earlier. Some of the early presidents were from this tradition.

The former grouping of predominantly Catholic Irish-Americans, lots of whom are several generations removed from this country, are regularly derided or even scorned by the people who were actually born and live here. These Hibernophiles look off in the distance through misty eyes in the direction of the 'auld sod' and identify themselves as Irish, though they have an American accent. They may or may not have paid a visit to the Emerald Isle, but many claim to feel a very real connection to it. And there is not a superlative in the dictionary that adequately sums up all that has emanated from that connection.

The close relationship between Ireland and the US is the envy of the world. For example, every other country would give just about anything to hear the new President of the

United States banter knowledgeably with a nominee to his cabinet about two of its sparsely populated, strategically irrelevant regions that they have ties to. But that is exactly what transpired when Joe Biden ribbed former Boston Mayor Marty Walsh, the son of Connemara emigrants, about the sporting and broader rivalry between Galway and Mayo when he announced that Walsh was his choice to be US Secretary of Labour. No matter how overly sentimental or downright schmaltzy his pronouncements may occasionally be, Ireland is fortunate in all sorts of tangible and intangible ways that Joe Biden is the American president.

While there have been repeated attempts to define or pigeonhole Irish-America, in 2021 it is a heterogeneous entity that has undergone myriad changes and is still evolving. Arguably the sole commonality within its membership is an affinity for Ireland at some level. They are massive in number. Between 30 and 40 million Americans assert that they are ethnically Irish. It should come as no surprise that they can't be tied down. That Irish-America has continued to transform itself presents a challenge for an Ireland that has likewise morphed into something quite new. And it is vital that we who are so committed to the preservation and deepening of a mutually beneficial and sacred friendship constantly update our understanding of who we are on both sides of the Atlantic. This is not an easy task, and it is one that will prove more complex as two seemingly inexorable trends in Ireland and Irish-America further play out. The first is the collective, though admittedly not uniform, shift in our politics and worldview. The second is the slow to a trickle in historic terms of the flow of individuals and families between our two countries, which always had been the safety valve for Ireland and was the genesis of Irish-America.

As the vast majority in Ireland reviled Donald Trump and his presidency, they were astonished at the number of devotees with Irish surnames who floated in and out of his inner circle. Conway, Kelly, McEnany, Mulvaney and Bannon are just a sampling. And Trump's deeply conservative vice-president, Mike Pence, had a grandfather who was born in Tubbercurry, County Sligo and great-grandparents from Doonbeg, County Clare, where his former boss took over a golf resort and is persistently popular among the locals as a consequence. Many here wondered at how these Irish-Americans could have forgotten about the widespread discrimination against those who preceded them. How could they collude with an avowedly anti-immigrant president when previous generations to the US had ultimately made a better life, but not before they were confronted by posters bearing hate-fuelled slogans like 'no Irish need apply'?

For them, the Democratic Party quickly became a natural home because it stood against hatred and bigotry and in favour of ordinary workers' rights in the face of the wealthy and often nativist-oriented employers who profited from their labour. This is how and why my Irish-American family and many others became involved in politics. At one stage, Irish-America was almost exclusively Democratic. The apex of that symbiotic affiliation came when one of their own, John F. Kennedy, was elected president in 1960. Although JFK was the scion of a rich and powerful family that had managed to gain partial entry to the elite establishment, it was a landmark moment nonetheless. It also marked the end of an era in which the party had a near-total hold on the support of Irish-America.

Two things happened. First, Irish-Americans did fantastically well and swiftly scaled the socio-economic ladder. As they did, they started to warm to the Republican mantra of lower taxes, especially insofar as it could help them to meet the rising expenses of their children's education or to get a second home in enclaves on Long Island or Cape Cod. They accepted the lines put out by Ronald Reagan and others in the GOP that the Democrats were the party of 'welfare mothers' and others who did not work for a living and tired of paying for others' upkeep. The statistics have never actually borne this out, yet it was provocative and persuasive. I know plenty, even in liberal Massachusetts, who have bought into it and are staunch Republicans. Some are relations and close friends. I even went along with it myself, for a time.

Second, and in my analysis an even bigger factor in the conversion, was the Democrats' move to the left on cultural issues and, in particular, the party's strenuous backing of permissive abortion laws. In the US, the people usually referred to elsewhere as Irish-Americans are perhaps better known as Irish Catholics. They tend – again, it is folly to try and paint them all into the same corner – to be more observant in their faith and practice of Catholicism, and all that entails, than the Irish are now. A great many are opposed to abortion and find it hard to reconcile the Democratic Party's advocacy for the most vulnerable and marginalised in society with its endorsement of legal abortion with almost no restrictions.

Lots of them have joined the old enemy for this reason. And I could not count the number of Irish-American Democrats I know who only vote with any enthusiasm for anti-abortion Democrats, a dwindling species, and routinely leave the ballot paper blank when faced with an unpalatable choice between a left-wing Democrat and a right-wing Republican. Moreover, the reverence for Catholic tradition transcends politics. For instance, back in the day, I can remember hearing of (and one would have heard about them in hushed tones) no more than a handful of weddings of hundreds of contemporaries from my East Milton neighbourhood that took place outside of a Catholic Church or following which the woman did not take the man's surname.

In a similar fashion, Ireland and its citizens have enjoyed significant economic success in recent decades. It is hard to tell whether it is concomitant, or merely concurrent, but the country has also erected some firm boundaries to separate itself from a Catholic Church that had dominated since the foundation of the state and has left a legacy that is shameful in some respects. It is hard for most Americans to fathom the degree of ubiquitous control the Church exerted. There is literally no aspect of Irish life in which it didn't feature prominently. And we now know how some of the clergy who Catholics were commanded to nearly deify and others in positions of authority committed unspeakable deeds and inflicted scars on survivors that will never fully heal. The damage that was done to so many who didn't deserve it, in concert with expanded access to higher education and the financial prosperity engendered by it and some prescient strategic decisions taken by governments over time – such as joining the European Economic Community and making Ireland a global hub for multinational corporations – helped ensure there would be a break with the Church.

The numbers don't lie. In the early 1980s, almost 90% of Irish Catholics attended Mass every week. Now, just over a third of us go. In the meantime, divorce was legalised by a narrow margin in a 1995 referendum over the opposition of the Catholic bishops, whose statements then held sway over a still-sizable chunk of the electorate. Same-sex marriage and the repeal of the 8th Amendment on abortion followed in the past several years. The Church hierarchy urged a No vote on both, but did so in a muted way, cognisant of its increasing irrelevance and the reality that injecting itself into the debate was more likely to hinder than help the cause. The 'Catholic Ireland' many Irish-Americans found solace in as their erstwhile allies in the Democratic Party turned on them was no more in a sense. With the caveat that I am relaying anecdotes, I know that some were angered and disappointed by the volte-face. 'That's just the way it is everywhere now, my family over there all voted for abortion,' an elderly emigrant with just a trace of a Cork accent left told me with no pleasure in a Boston area Irish pub.

So there is Ireland and Irish-America – the former eagerly discarding the constraints of Catholic conservatism and the latter holding on to the old ways – leftist 'heretics' vs conservative 'relics'. As ever, it's tempting to portray it that simplistically. But there are lots of liberal Irish-Americans. A strong contingent of them serves in the upper echelons of the Biden Administration. The president himself, though a practising Catholic, used one of his first executive orders to restore US government funding to overseas non-profit organisations that provide abortions. On the flip side, notwithstanding the decline of belief and practice here, almost 80% of Irish people call themselves Catholics and attendance at Mass, in percentage terms, is far in excess of the European average.[16]

It is vital, however, that residents of the old and new country understand one another, allowing for the fact that there are areas where they legitimately and passionately disagree. On this side, it is important to recognise that Irish identity and Catholic identity were intrinsically intertwined and something that made those who claimed both stand out in a diverse and secular country. Their experience is vastly different to that of those who have only known living alongside people who are cut from the same cloth. As such, it ought to come as no surprise that Irish-Americans cherish what separated them from the rest. Additionally, insofar as Irish-Americans have gravitated toward the Republican Party's traditional vision of low taxes and small government, they are only a reflection of the US. The country's model puts incentivising individuals to maximise their opportunities to succeed and prosper ahead of the well-being of society writ large. With very mixed results, the model presumes that the second imperative is improved by the first.

Although some are very well acquainted with it, many Irish-Americans would do well to obtain a better appreciation of recent Irish history. Whether it is about the activities of the

16 2016 Census Data available at https://www.cso.ie/en/releasesandpublications/ep/p-cp8iter/p8iter/p8rrc/ <last accessed 14 May 2021>; Patsy McGarry, 'Ireland still one of the most Christian states in Europe', *The Irish Times*, 4 June 2018, available at https://www.irishtimes.com/news/social-affairs/ireland-still-one-of-the-most-christian-states-in-europe-1.3518269 <last accessed 14 May 2021>.

provisional IRA that are romanticised in the ballads that blare in Irish pubs, the nature of life in modern Ireland or the way the young Irish perceive the US, something of a time warp persists. Most of those here who can remember the Troubles loathe the IRA. Modern Ireland is just that, forward and outward thinking to an extent that much of America is not and no longer bound by religious doctrine. And though some Irish young women and men remain keen to live the American Dream, they are equally likely to look askance at a country that is so conservative and splintered and select continental Europe, Australia, New Zealand or Canada as their top destinations for holidays or to spend a lengthier spell. A religious faith that millions of Irish-Americans are grateful for instead took the shape of an oppressive, malevolent institution in the lives of countless Irish people.

This is not the Ireland of Irish-Americans' parents, grandparents, great-grandparents or further removed antecedents. Not even close. That said, Ireland forever looks to America. The very reason that the Irish were so aggrieved by the Trump presidency was that they expect a lot more from a country they are so close to. One could say that there is hypocrisy in Irish people defending their static version of the US, while they simultaneously lampoon Irish-Americans who prefer to live in the past. Nonetheless, they are daring to dream that all that they had thought was great about America can be rediscovered, resuscitated and re-imagined. Many are acting accordingly.

The Irish and their American cousins have changed over the years. It is only natural and should not really pose a big threat to the relationship between the two countries as long as we continue to update our understandings of each other. This is crucial. In this vein, it is encouraging that Irish-Americans are learning more about today's Ireland through extensive global media coverage of milestone referendums and that Irish politicians are cultivating friendships with conservative Republicans with a grá for this island. A huge impediment, however, sprung up as major changes manifested themselves. That is the pressing of the pause button on legal Irish immigration to the US. And this has precipitated a challenge of even greater proportions to all that we rightly celebrate. How do we preserve what the movement of people has made when people can no longer move?

The number of Americans claiming Irish ancestry has declined by several million since the start of the century. Census data shows that, while there were more than 250,000 US residents who were born in Ireland in 1980, there are about 150,000 at present. While Irish immigration to the US was heavy in the 1950s and 1960s, with another bump in the 1980s and 1990s thanks to my Uncle Brian's visa and the Morrison programme that succeeded it, only about 1,000 Irish people obtain US citizenship or permission to remain permanently each year. I can see and hear it when I am back in Boston. It's not the same as it used to be. Again, the majority of my friends had at least one parent who hailed from the west of Ireland. Irish bars and restaurants were everywhere and the bar and wait staff were all Irish. If you wanted work done on your house, the builders were almost invariably Irish, and county loyalties came into play when selecting a plumber, roofer, carpenter or electrician.

Tricolours, as well as maroon and white Galway flags, green and red Mayo flags et al., commonly flew next to the stars and stripes outside houses and businesses.

That Irishness is still there, but it's not as omnipresent. Dorchester Avenue and Quincy Centre are no longer filled with rough and ready Irish gin mills. There are a few, but many Irish bar owners have sold up or opened new, more upscale establishments in the suburbs on the city's south shore, nicknamed the 'Irish Riviera' long ago because it was where successful Irish-Americans decamped to from cramped city neighbourhoods. At any rate, the Irish-America – with a strong emphasis on Irish – that I grew up in is unlikely to be replicated. Unless immigration laws are comprehensively amended, those who grow up in the Boston area in future will have an experience that is akin to Joe Biden's Scranton, a more distant Irishness with a heavy American accent. And those whose formative years are spent in Scranton will have a more indistinguishably American childhood and adolescence. In some ways, the US is becoming less Irish. There won't be as many with a birthright to the two passports we nearly took for granted.

Some look at what has transpired and conclude that Irish-America is on life support – that its influence in politics and other spheres has diminished greatly and that Irish people who think it really matters are indulging a fantasy. I strenuously reject their dire prophesies and am appalled that they apparently are not too bothered by what they see as the slow death of the community that I am so proud to be a product of. Their negativity, however, is instructive insofar as it illustrates that efforts need to be redoubled as demographics begin to work against us. The work and enthusiasm on this front are actually quite extraordinary. The one thing Irish-America's sceptics tend to underplay is that being Irish is cool in the US in 2021. When I was younger, contemporaries whose parents' words betrayed the fact that they weren't from Boston tried their best to keep them away and were nearly ashamed of them. That is no longer the case if the plethora of county jerseys worn by young American-born boys and girls I see in East Milton and thereabouts or the unbridled joy I see in their faces as we get on board the same Aer Lingus plane at Logan Airport is anything to go by.

The Irish are America's favourite Europeans. And as with everything Irish, the Gaelic Athletic Association is playing a huge part. The GAA is remarkable in the way it creates and strengthens bonds. And the GAA's tentacles are deeply embedded throughout the US. When I am home, it is heartening to see familiar goalposts in the parks where I played baseball, basketball and football as a boy. My hometown GAA youth club, Trinity Milton, is thriving, as are clubs throughout Massachusetts. Even in places where there are not as many Irish, the GAA has been adopted by families who love its amateur ethos and are fascinated by the games. And Irish culture has made lasting inroads. Irish festivals attract massive crowds from Milwaukee to Florida. The curiosity this all arouses is expanding the fertile territory that can be built upon.

Business ties are also flourishing. Everyone knows that Ireland is a European hub for multinational corporations, particularly in the tech sector. Yet many should be aware that Irish businesses employ thousands of Americans at their hubs that are scattered around the US. The Irish government has been to the fore on this front. Additionally, the Irish government has wisely funded initiatives around the US in order to foster attachment as the bonds of blood loosen. The inclusion of Irish history and of the Irish-American experience is the most promising of these. Irish Studies is a well-recognised academic discipline with Irish and Irish-American scholars educating young people about the Ireland of today and how they integrated into the US. A cadre of experts is sharing their insights about the US with Irish students. Educational exchange programmes, in particular, according to former Taoiseach Bertie Ahern and other stakeholders, are core ingredients to reinvigorating the vitality of our relationship. Knowing more about each other will engender sympathetic, well-informed citizens here and there who will use the positions of authority they will be in to continually bolster our alliance.

And the quest to allow more Irish young people to pursue lives and livelihoods in the US has not ended. Notwithstanding the contention of detractors that Irish-America is a dead letter with next to no pull on Capitol Hill, the Congressional Friends of Ireland keep pushing it, emboldened by having a former member of their caucus in the White House. The present chair of the group, Richard Neal of Springfield, Massachusetts, is simultaneously the chair of the House Ways and Means Committee. As an important aside, it is worth reiterating that Brexit has galvanised Irish-American politicians of all stripes in defence of the Good Friday Agreement. Through the effective intercessions of Neal, Congressman Brendan Boyle and other champions, a rarely unified US Congress has sent a clear message to the United Kingdom as to how important peace and stability on this island are in the corridors of power in Washington. And President Biden is with them all the way.

Returning to immigration, The Congressional Friends of Ireland are pushing for the Irish to be allowed to access unused E3 visas that are annually set aside for Australians. I believe this will be accomplished and should pave a path to US citizenship for several hundred Irish men and women every year. When and if it is, Irish-Americans, such as Niall O'Dowd and Ciaran Staunton, and Irish politicians, such as Senator Mark Daly and former Senator Billy Lawless, should take a bow for their work over many years.

It would be an incremental victory to be sure, yet it is important to remember that the effective discrimination against putative Irish immigrants to the US that the Donnelly and Morrison visas sought to mitigate persists. Again, even as the sceptics bizarrely dismiss it out of hand with gusto, there is still a compelling case for Irish-specific immigration reform. Lastly, the tens of thousands of undocumented Irish have genuine cause for optimism in light of President Biden's plan to regularise the status of millions of illegal immigrants. I believe the president is fully committed to aiding these mainly Hispanic people because of the way those who came to America before them are finding an unlikely political home in the Republican Party. He needs to do something to bring them back. Whatever the genesis, a rising tide lifts all boats in this instance.

Something that has been overlooked when it comes to the movement of people is allowing for Americans with Irish connections to live and work here. The laws are extremely restrictive. The Irish government should make it easier for Irish-Americans who wish to live in Ireland for a time, especially given that the slowing of immigration means that the numbers of us who are entitled to an Irish passport by birth will shrink. On every visit back to Boston, I meet Irish-Americans who elicit my story and then tell me how jealous they are. Hearing about the relatively trifling cost of higher education invariably excites the parents of young children. The growth in remote working ushered in by COVID-19 and the globalised economy makes this a realistic possibility for scores of Irish-Americans and means that they would not necessarily be taking jobs away from Irish people when they relocate here. It is something that should be considered and acted on.

All in all, it would be foolhardy to deny that things have changed and will continue to do so. But I am resolutely positive and hopeful about the enduring vitality of the treasured relationship between the two nations I will forever call home with the deepest pride imaginable. There are so many of us who are vested in this relationship and are committed to doing everything within our power to preserve what is the envy of the rest of the world. Its fullest expression can be seen every March when the prime minister of this relatively tiny country has a bilateral meeting with the President of the United States on St. Patrick's Day. It is a time to take stock and for the Irish at home and the Irish that have made America their new home to update their understandings of one another. I believe the constant updating of our understandings is the key to maintaining what we have.

Afterword:
Parting Thoughts from a
Unique Vantage Point

If anyone had told me in August of 1999 that I would spend the bulk of the next two decades in Ireland, I would have laughed him or her out of the room. I had graduated from law school near the top of my class, had just sat the Massachusetts bar exam and was set to commence a job at a respected law firm in downtown Boston. All was right with the world and I was set to realise the ambitions that I had worked so hard for. In common with many young people, I didn't really know what I wanted and quickly discovered that I didn't want what I thought I wanted. Then, the trip I made to Galway in April of 2000 – where I had not been since 1986, when I was 11 – opened my eyes and changed the trajectory of my life.

It made me aware that there was a world beyond Boston and outside the US. That might sound obvious to people who aren't from Boston and don't get how insular we tend to be.

It is a big deal that I left it behind. I did so because I loved Ireland pretty much instantly. I didn't want to leave it at the end of that vacation and it was on my mind thereafter. When would I get back and could I make use of my Irish passport to live and work there? Fortunately, I have been able to do just that. Occasionally, I wonder how things would have turned out had I stayed in Boston. Maybe I'm wrong, but I can't imagine that I would be happy or fulfilled – either personally or professionally.

Ireland is a great place. Of course, it has changed for the better and for the worse, yet there are still the little things that are actually the big things and that make life here wonderful to me. The glorious scenery. The GAA. The friendliness that is instinctive and infectious. The prevalent sense of solidarity and the willingness to help those who are in need, which were so refreshing during the pandemic. The special connection with America, and the familiarity with my home territory especially. The refusal to take anyone or anything too seriously and the corollary scorn for those who have notions. Long afternoons in the pub or on the golf course. I could go on with the sentimentality. This is how I feel, however. And unlike millions of wistful fellow Irish-Americans, I have lived it and am a part of it. I speak from experience.

I don't think about it very much, yet it is quite something that my family left the west of Ireland and did very well in Boston and I have made the reverse journey. As my father used to remind me, 'Your grandmother would be praying for you to come to your senses and questioning your sanity if she knew you were back in Galway.' But Ireland has been my land of opportunity. Forging a career in legal academia probably would have been impossible in that the American professoriate is largely reserved for alumni of a handful of elite law schools. Having a hugely rewarding avocation as a political pundit in the national and local media would have been the stuff of dreams in all likelihood. Meeting and marrying a woman like Eileen Whelan would not have happened. I will forever consider myself lucky.

I do think a lot about the opportunities that my sons will have. Seán is 22 and in the final year of a business degree at Technological University Dublin. He will emerge with no debt and the option of working anywhere in the US or in Europe. He intends to undertake an MBA part-time in a few years. While Larry Óg is only eight, the same doors will be open to him and we should be able to ensure that he is not burdened with educational debt, regardless of which avenue he chooses to pursue. What they take for granted contrasts so drastically with the situation that will be faced by their contemporaries in America, many of whose existences will be shackled by staggering monthly loan repayments. Travelling the world and postgraduate study sadly will not be feasible for them.

To be frank, their plight makes me sick. It also makes me angry when I hear the 'America is the land of opportunity' mantra repeated unthinkingly over and over. For the wealthy, including some of my closest friends, paying for third-level tuition doesn't present a major difficulty. Cutting a cheque in excess of $30,000 twice a year is not a bother to the super rich. Their kids don't know how good they have it. The children of teachers, nurses, police officers are in an altogether different position. Their parents work hard and do jobs that are arguably the most important to having a cohesive society and a properly functioning country. But because they do, their children will begin their adult lives at a serious disadvantage. And in most instances, their parents need to scrimp, save and sacrifice as best they can from the moment their daughters and sons are born to ameliorate the trap that awaits them. It is my own sons, and my namesake in particular, who I have in mind when I am asked – as I frequently am – whether I could be tempted to move back to the US.

In good conscience, I could not do so unless I either won a huge lottery jackpot or had a job offer with a salary in the high six figures. That is the only way I could guarantee that Larry could obtain a good undergraduate degree without a gargantuan debt hanging over him. Of all the problems that the US desperately needs to reckon with, I am convinced that the preposterous cost of higher education is the worst. A qualification is the passport to financial security and the obstacles to obtaining a college or university diploma are substantial. This is a recipe for income inequality. If the rest of the world can facilitate access to degree courses without crippling young men and women, why can't America? It may be because I work in a university, but looking back across the Atlantic, this is what I despair at above all.

I do still love America. I treasure my holidays in Boston with my family. Seeing the Boston skyline from the window of an Aer Lingus plane as we taxi to the terminal literally sends shivers down my spine. It will always occupy a special place in my heart. It is great to see my wife and sons interact with my relatives and lifelong friends in Boston, who have been so welcoming to them. Bringing them to my favourite eateries and hostelries is equally a joy.

And I get a kick out of chance encounters in their presence with the guys and girls from East Milton who've known me since we were frightened, insecure little kids figuring out what life is all about. The other end of the conversation typically goes something like this: 'Howahya, Lah? How's everything over there? My cousins in (insert one of the following) Galway/Connemara/Mayo/Donegal say they hear you on the radio all the time. Respected political commentator, who are you f**kin' kiddin'? (Turning to my wife) I remember the time when … OK maybe I shouldn't tell that story! Great to see you back in town.' We will never let one another get too big for our britches and, while I have formed some terrific friendships in Ireland, there is something truly special about the friends you've known since childhood.

But the changes in America are evident in East Milton, too. The price of real estate is off the charts. It is exceedingly rare to see a property for sale for less than half a million dollars. In a sense, newcomers are drawn by what we equally cherished and assumed was our birthright. It is a stone's throw, in relative terms, on the subway or in a car from downtown Boston and a vibrant community with great schools and abundant activities for kids. Milton justifiably ranks among the most attractive towns to live in in the US. It makes me sad, however, that my family and the vast majority of my friends' families could not afford to live there today. I don't bear any ill will toward newcomers who are contributing greatly to the town, yet its character (and its Irishness), what made it the place I am so proud to be a native of, is being diluted. And the same goes for many of Boston's neighbourhoods and close-in suburbs. The middle class has been displaced by people with higher incomes. Even above-average earners are being pushed further and further out from the city or area they identify with. The same process of gentrification is going on across the country.

The inequality is palpable in the city as well. Well-to-do lawyers and businesspeople think little of paying $10 for a pint of Guinness or glass of wine in the Irish pubs that dot the financial district, Beacon Hill and Faneuil Hall. Meanwhile, women and men – predominantly people of colour, many of them immigrants, some of them undocumented – stand ready to serve behind the counters of the delis where the professionals get their sandwiches or clean their offices for an hourly wage that is not much more than the price of a single after-work drink.

I understand that this is the way of the world in 2021, but in America it is so tangible and so unquestioned. There is an epidemic of inequality. It is vulgar. Perhaps this state of play wouldn't make me so uncomfortable if I hadn't emigrated and merely accepted this by-product of forces well beyond my control. Yet it is one of the things I find most disturbing on my visits there. Although income inequality is an issue in Ireland, I am heartened by the statistical data revealing that the gap between rich and poor has diminished and by the fact that our progressive tax code militates against disparity. Additionally, unlike in the US, I can't recall hearing an elected official either endeavouring to defend or to actively collude in socio-economic stratification.

That having been said, in Massachusetts and elsewhere across the country, the concerted move to the left of my Democratic Party has not contributed much to levelling the playing field. In some ways, the city of Boston is a case study in this regard. An enormous amount has been written and said about how Boston has been transformed utterly since the dark days of forced busing. And it has. The city is now minority-majority and far more fully integrated. There are no politicians who remotely resemble populists like John Kerrigan, Elvira 'Pixie' Palladino or Louise Day Hicks who held office during busing and thrived on racial tension. The school committee is no longer an elected body and is comprised of appointed education experts. The city council is more than 50% female and there are numerous councillors of colour. Martin Walsh may have been an Irish-American mayor whose parents hailed from Connemara and who looked and sounded like the personification of 'old Boston', yet he is miles to the left of his predecessors.

Boston is a forward-thinking, progressive city where countless people would love to live and lots of born and bred Bostonians would love to stay. But they can't. The formerly working-class neighbourhoods of South Boston, Charlestown and Dorchester have been taken over by rich outsiders to the point that they are unaffordable for most. I have heard stories here from Irish people who talk about homes they owned there before coming back having increased tenfold or more in price in the course of a decade or so. Income inequality, not racial strife and division, is the biggest crisis facing the city at the moment. The challenge for a new breed of Boston politicians is to solve it. This will necessitate bold, outside the box, perhaps anti-capitalist thinking and consequent action. It will require that they say no to the developers who are in it to make money and regularly write big cheques to politicians who do their bidding. The new Bostonians they serve – and the old Bostonians who despair at the direction of things – deserve no less. I will be monitoring developments there in hope and with keen interest.

While I love America and Ireland, for all of the foregoing reasons and more besides, I have voted with my feet. I adore Boston, but it has become a place I relish visiting. Ireland is where I live. And it is precisely because of how I feel about Ireland that, when asked if I would consider entering the political fray here, I say that I would never close that door. Politics is in my blood. It is what I know and what animates much of my thinking from the moment I wake until I go to bed. It is my passion. I believe with every fibre of my being that politics is a noble profession and that, through political activism, people's lives can be changed for the better. If the timing and the circumstances were right and if Eileen, Seán and Larry Óg were supportive, I would strongly consider it. I believe I have something to contribute.

At any rate, *sin é* from me. Suffice it to say that my life hasn't followed the path I thought it would. Far from it. I still laugh at my teenage self who regarded going forty-odd miles from home to attend college as the equivalent of a mission to outer space! Now, I am 3,000 miles from Boston, and I wouldn't trade where I am or my experience of getting here for anything. It has been wonderful and unique in so many ways.

Afterword

In the end, I am privileged to call the United States of America and Ireland my homes. And with my family, I look forward to writing the next chapters in this transatlantic odyssey.

Acknowledgements

Writing a book like this is something that I had long thought about and discussed informally with friends and colleagues over the years. It only came to be after I conducted a public interview with RTÉ's former Washington correspondent and current Six One News anchor Caitríona Perry in November 2019 at the US Embassy in Dublin. Deirdre Nolan of Gill Books, who published Caitríona's two books, approached me shortly thereafter, just before COVID-19 arrived in Ireland, with the idea for *The Bostonian*.

As such, I am hugely grateful to Deirdre, to Teresa Daly, Aoibheann Molumby and all the team at Gill Books, as well as to Sheila Armstrong, a superb editor, for helping me get *The Bostonian* over the line. I would also like to thank Caitríona and her colleague at RTÉ, Rachael English, both of whom are accomplished authors and who generously offered me valuable advice before I began writing.

To tell my story properly, it was essential that I draw upon the perspectives of experts and high-profile individuals who were, in some cases, central protagonists in the events detailed herein. Accordingly, I am grateful to the following people for spending so much time with me and sharing their stories and insights: former Boston City Councillor and chronicler of the city's political history, Larry DiCara; former Taoiseach Bertie Ahern; *Irish Voice* publisher and IrishCentral.com founder Niall O'Dowd; former European Commissioner, Minister for Justice and Galway West TD (among other things) Máire Geoghegan-Quinn; and James Sharkey, political counsellor in the Irish Embassy in Washington, DC during the 1980s and later Ireland's ambassador to several different nations.

In this vein, I especially must pay tribute to my uncle and godfather, Brian Donnelly. One of the things I most wanted to do in *The Bostonian* is to tell the extraordinary story of his career in politics and government. Brian doesn't seek media attention or court popular acclaim – never has, never will. I thought he would be hesitant to allow me to write at length about what I believe are his outstanding accomplishments as a public servant. But he couldn't have been more obliging or frank in our numerous, wide-ranging conversations over many hours. I only hope I have done some justice to his legacy.

I want to acknowledge my colleagues in the School of Law and beyond at the National University of Ireland, Galway. NUIG is a great institution that I owe an awful lot to and whose affiliation I am very proud to be able to tout each and every time I engage in media debate and discourse in either Ireland or the US. In particular, I need to recognise the truly eminent Professor Gerard Quinn, who I regard as an honorary Bostonian, such is his grá for the city of my birth. Gerard took a chance on a young lawyer fresh out of Suffolk University Law School and a short-lived stint in law practice 20 years ago. I like to think his gamble paid off! I also have to thank my good friend, Professor Donncha O'Connell, for always being a great sounding board and the source of sage advice. He was one of the few who knew I was working on *The Bostonian* in my spare time and was his usual brilliant self throughout the process.

I am thankful to those who have given me a platform to share my thoughts and my rather unique vantage point in print for more than a decade now. First, Niall O'Dowd at IrishCentral.com invited me to write columns for their largely Irish-American audience, which were skilfully edited and shaped by Kate Hickey and others in New York and in Dublin. Since late in 2012, I have been a regular columnist for TheJournal.ie, Ireland's leading online news source. I am grateful to Editors Susan Daly and Sinéad O'Carroll, to Deputy Editor Christine Bohan and, above all, to Laura Byrne, the Opinion Editor who has the frequent (mis)fortune of meticulously reading my work. It is a privilege to have a column in TheJournal every second week. And latterly, courtesy of the kind intercession of Ed Forry, a quintessential local journalist, I have been reconnecting with my hometown's still-vibrant Irish community in *Boston Irish* magazine.

Avid readers of my columns will recognise similarities between my past writings and some of what appears in *The Bostonian*. This was unavoidable. In this regard, Chapter Two on the tumultuous era of forced busing in Boston draws heavily from an essay I wrote – 'Busing in Boston and Senator Edward Kennedy' – in *From Whence I Came: The Kennedy Legacy, Ireland and America*, which was edited by Dr Brian

Murphy and Professor Donnacha Ó Beacháin and published by Merrion Press earlier in 2021.

The Kennedy Summer School has been another means of indulging my love for politics and was a further source of inspiration for this book. From my involvement in the summer school, I have gained another Irish home place – New Ross – and made lots of friends. I want to offer my gratitude to friends and colleagues on the KSS organising committee: Brian Murphy, Willie Keilthy, Eileen Dunne, Bob Mauro, Eamonn Hore and Sinéad McSweeney. Of course, we dearly miss Sinéad's late husband, Noel Whelan, who founded the Kennedy Summer School.

I want to thank the extended Donnelly and Flanigan families stateside who feature in *The Bostonian*, as well as the Murphy family in the wondrous west of Ireland. The Murphys may be distant relations technically, yet have become like first cousins and were so instrumental to my settling in to life in Ireland.

With one or two exceptions and even though they are immensely important to my life, I do not name close friends in this book. Because I would never hear the end of it if I did not signify how much they all mean to me, I promised to include them here (if I missed you, you know who you are!): in Galway, Fergus McGinn and the entire McGinn clan and Keith Greally and his family, especially my godson Rían; in Gorey, Pat 'the Bear' Masterson; and here in Wicklow, all of the many, many Whelan in-laws (although they are spread around the world), great neighbours, and friends from Wicklow Golf Club, local hostelries, etc. I should also remember some of the crew who ensured that my four years as an undergraduate at the College of the Holy Cross were pretty damn funny and often ridiculous: Danny Joyce, Dave Devine, Tony Earle, Bob Jenney, Matt McClane, Dave Walker, Matt Walsh, Tom Stevens, etc., as well as my friends from the *Suffolk Transnational Law Review* who helped to make law school a pleasure.

And near to my heart, my lifelong pals from East Milton or thereabouts. We will never disown the place – to us, it's 'God's country' – we are so lucky to be from. Tim Jewell, Florin 'FMan' Neamtu, Jim Kennedy, Brian Naughton, Mike McDonnell, Mike Nellany, Jeff Nellany, Timmy McDonnell, Dennis Punch, Eric Phelan, Matt Brennan, etc. Notwithstanding our manifest flaws as human beings, we have managed to marry and build strong relationships with better people. Their wives, partners, close friends and children have become equally valued members of an ever-expanding inner circle.

I mention them all not just because I love them, but because they are a big part of my story.

My brother Tommy, my sister-in-law Jesse and my nephew and godson Tommy have always been there for me and were so good in recent years to my dad as his condition worsened. It was not easy for them and I wish I could have been there to help more. I love them dearly and wish we could be together more often. The days the Donnellys/Whelans spend with them back in East Milton or the vacations on which they visit us are incredibly special. Additionally, I am in their debt for finding the wonderful photo that graces the cover of *The Bostonian* in a box in the cellar at 14 Sheldon Street, where I grew up and they live.

Lastly, a couple of lines for my own family. Seán eagerly accepted an outsider who was competing for his mother's previously undivided attention and affection in 2008 at the tender age of eight. That he did is testament to the quality of his character and an uncommon maturity. That he has continued to put up with me since is actually astounding. Larry Óg is the centre of my universe. I never thought I could love anyone the way I love him. I only pray he keeps growing even taller, keeps swinging the golf club better than his dad does and will soon decide that he enjoys going to school and attending Mass!

Meeting Eileen Whelan was the best thing that has ever happened to me. In one sense, it's a pity that she can't share more of herself when she is reading the news on RTÉ. I can guarantee that most of the rest of the country would soon be as enamoured of her as I am if she did. I never thought I'd have a family life like we do; I'm equally thrilled and comforted every day in the knowledge that Eileen loves me.

All in all, I know that Mum and Dad are smiling at how things have turned out. I owe it to them.

Larry Donnelly
Wicklow Town
Summer 2021